Single, Celibate & Dating

A Guide for the Celibate Single & Abstinent Couple

Chloe M. Gooden

Single, Celibate & Dating
Copyright 2016 Chloe M. Gooden
All rights reserved.

ISBN-13: 978-1533660152
ISBN-10: 1533660158
Also available in eBook
Cover Design:
Author Photo: Daria Blevins
Cover Design: Vanessa Mendozzi
Interior Design: Sandeep Likhar

Need answers or advice? Message Me on Facebook @
https://www.facebook.com/ChloeMGooden

Table of Contents

Introduction

S ex. Sex. Sex. I don't know about you, but I get sick of hearing about it. It is seriously everywhere; magazines, commercials, books, tv, Instagram, and Snapchat... everywhere! You cannot escape sex no matter where you go. I remember a time when the only way you could see something sexual on tv was in the late night hours, and you had to be watching a specific cable channel. These days, you will see sex on daytime television. Beyond it being advertised everywhere, people are being introduced to the subject of sex a lot earlier in their lives. For me, I don't remember being presented with the topic of sex until high school. Now, kids are aware of what sex is while they are in elementary school. It is truly appalling. At that age, I still remember boys and girls thinking they had the cooties. Kids don't send love letters and "Do you like me?" notes anymore. No, they send naked pictures and invites for Netflix and Chill. We see it so much that we have become numb to the subject. Furthermore, we don't think of it as a big deal or as something to pay too much attention to. Why should we? Everyone is doing it and its fun, liberating and part of a relationship. One of the best parts! We can't even imagine going into a relationship with the thought of not having sex. That's crazy. It's hard even to imagine ignoring the subject, especially in relationships. So even contemplating the thought of not having sex as a couple is hard to imagine. We feel it is a part of a relationship and some even feel it's not a relationship unless you are having sex. We act as if sex consummates the relationship as official and the relationship is only deemed as a friendship or dating without it. It's as if sex is a part of the relationship contract. But it is not, it is a part of the marriage covenant.

But it seems some things are beginning to change. Though at one point we could never imagine having a relationship without sex, it seems that now, ironically, the more sex seems to be a huge deal; many people are deciding to stop having sex. What?! Surprising right? Oh, how I wish this were a new "fad" when I was younger. It would have been a lot easier to date! I wish it were popular to wait for marriage and it not seem obscure to want to wait. I remember when I was dating, if I told a guy I wanted to wait for marriage, they would immediately label me as the "good girl" or "old fashioned." This usually happened to any girl that was seen as doing this crazy thing called waiting. Every guy always knew the girl that wanted to wait. They wouldn't even attempt to date you. Now for some reason, it is now seen as the new thing. To wait.

I have noticed over the past couple of years many couples have decided to wait for marriage to have sex. From Meaghan Good and Devon Franklin to Ciara and Russel

Wilson, couples are displaying to the world their decision to wait for marriage. But they're not the only people who have waited or waiting, for marriage to have sex. Tamera Mowry, Jennifer Hudson, Tim Tebow, Jordin Sparks, and even Lenny Kravitz say they want to or did wait, until marriage to have sex. Now you start to wonder, why is it people are deciding to wait? What happened? Why, out of nowhere, are people feeling that this is a pretty good idea? I mean, at first, it was all about being free, having sex and enjoying life! It was all about women being able to do the same as men and being promiscuous. It was all about making your own decision to have sex with the one you love. Sew your wild oats! Now ironically people are praising the life of waiting. So you have to wonder, what has changed? Why such a different tone when it comes to the world and sex? Let's look at some common reasons many of the popular couples state why they are waiting as well as ordinary couples.

- To be free emotionally, spiritually and physically.
- To show a level of discipline and honor to God.
- To focus more on getting to know their partner and not only seek them physically.
- To maintain peace and purity in their relationship.
- To present their partner pure before God.
- To see if they truly love the person without sex.
- To be the man to lead the woman righteously.
- To truly know if they are the one.
- To not be distracted by sex.
- To make our wedding night special.

- To start their relationship the right way.

There are multiple reasons why some have decided to wait, but these are just a few. Everyone will have their reasons as to why they are waiting for marriage and I am sure you have your own as well. *(I will discuss the importance of this later in the book.)* So where did this idea of waiting come from? Is this a new idea? Of course, not. You know whose idea it was first? God's. God has been telling us for ages to wait until marriage to have sex. Ages! Yet, it took people in celebrity status for us to finally stop and think, "Hmm. Maybe this is a good idea. Maybe they are on to something?" It's actually pretty funny, but sadly that's how we are. It takes someone in high power and status before we start paying attention to certain things.

God created us and created sex, yet it takes us first hearing it from a celebrity before we contemplate making a change in our dating life. Why would we not listen to the author and creator of sex? Why would we not listen to the one who knows literally everything? I think some of it is caused by the way the Bible, and sex is presented in the church. Let me explain this a little bit more from my own experience.

My Journey

Making the decision to wait for marriage was definitely a hard decision for me to make and I honestly struggled with it a lot after I had sex and decided to stop again. I waited for almost 24 years until I made the decision to have sex. For years I was so proud, I was able to keep my virginity, and I knew I would make it to marriage. Wrong! I can laugh about it now, but I honestly wish I could have waited. I know why I finally ended up having sex and it's something that I truly wish was taught more in the church, or by our parents, so others won't fall victim to it. In my mind, as long as I didn't have intercourse I wasn't having sex, and that's all that mattered. So, me being arrogant and prideful, I felt that I was still as pure as a bell and was doing just fine with my sexual life. Little did I know those "harmful" acts of foreplay and fantasies would lead me to have sex with a long time ex-boyfriend of mine. It was rare that you heard people trying to wait for marriage. As soon as I would tell a potential mate I was doing so they either said, 'Oh, that's cool. I respect that," or they claimed they were okay with it but didn't do anything to help the situation. A guy, unless he is an honest man, will not immediately let you know they aren't capable of waiting.

When I first started dating, I immediately would tell a guy that I was waiting for marriage. I thought that was the best way to handle it. Let them know up front so they know ahead of time. I quickly learned that was not the way to handle it. Regardless, we would continue to date, and the truth was eventually revealed. They may not have started out pushing for sex, but they would push for us to do everything but sex. Me being naïve, I was completely unaware that this was not okay. So I played with the idea of foreplay and anything else that wasn't "sex" in my eyes. If you were like me, I was only taught that sex, actual intercourse, was an issue. No one ever discussed everything else that came before sex to steer away from. When people discussed sex, it was only told to us that "It's a sin, and it is wrong. God said it's wrong, so don't do it." That's it. Beyond that, that was all I knew. So in my mind, anything else was up for grabs! Literally *(joking)*. Going from partner to partner I learned quickly that eventually you get tired of foreplay. You get tired of just kissing, touching, and all the rest. It's just like if you have always wanted to try ice cream, but someone tells you, you cannot have ice cream until you are 16. So when that person isn't around, you have frozen yogurt to suffice. Then you get tired of the frozen yogurt, and you decide to try sherbet. That gets old also. Then eventually you think to yourself, "Maybe I'll just taste the ice cream. Just lick it a little bit to see what it tastes like and I'll be fine." So you try the ice cream, its good, but you feel okay because you didn't actually eat the entire thing. Just a taste. So then you start trying different flavors. But you only take a lick or two. Then one day it gets old. It's not enough. You want more ice cream! So you take one lick. Two licks. Three licks, then boom, out of nowhere you have eaten all of the ice cream! You couldn't resist it. You were tired of just tasting it; you wanted it all. That's how it is with sex. You can try to play around with it all day, but eventually, you will end up doing it. It's innate in your body to do so. The best thing to do is stop before it even starts. I had this situation happen to my first partner and me and we eventually ended up having sex. After that, it was hard to stop. Very hard. Till this day, I wish someone would have told me why I should've waited, beyond the typical answer. I could have truly avoided so many heartaches and soul ties.

The entire reason why I am in ministry is to help others avoid these situations. I want to stop you before it starts. I want you to know why you should wait, how to do it and tips to keep you from making a decision you could regret. I know that sometimes it feels as if you are missing out on something. I know that sometimes you feel like what's the point or wonder if you will ever even get married. Or maybe you get mad at God wondering why He would wire you to want something so natural but not provide a way for you to release it? I get it. It can be so frustrating and hard to understand. I've been there, and I have asked God the same questions. But there is one thing you have to remember about God.

God was in the flesh as Jesus Christ. He knows, and He went through every temptation and was able to bear it and have victory in it. If I know anything, God will not ask us to do anything that is impossible. But what it does require is work. Jesus didn't just walk around, throw his hands up, and cause every temptation to flee. No, he had to fight. He had to remind the enemy of the Word of God. He was equipped with the armor to defeat temptation. He had a plan, and He executed it every time. You have to put your work with your faith. This is the thing, being celibate isn't easy. It's not. I am just being honest with you so that you know what lies ahead. But what I have learned, is that anything that is good for us is not easily attainable. It usually takes work and sacrifice. Though it is hard, I promise you it is so worth the fight. Anything that God asks us to do is to protect us and give us the best. He doesn't just go around throwing out demands just for the sake of it. That is not how He works. Everything He tells us to do is in our best interest and to give us the best life. That's what He wants for you. The best life. He loves you a lot. A lot! He gives us these guidelines because He created us and knew if we followed His guidelines we would be at our best!

Think about it. If you have a car, I am sure it came with a manual, right? Now people rarely read these things *(I never have either. Ha.)* though we should. Now this manual tells us everything about our car. What oil to put in it, what tire pressure is needed, mileage, what the signals mean, everything you can think of. It's there so we can get the best out of our car so that it can operate effectively. Did you ever think that the Bible works the same way? God gave us a guide. A spirit filled book to help give us the best life! That's it. But how many of us read the manual? How many of us take the time to actually apply God's tips? Many of us don't. But everything we need to know to have a fulfilling life is in His Word! So please go into this with an open mind. He is not trying to punish you, but to save you. Save you from unnecessary heartaches, ties and regrets. When I realized everything God instructs us to do is out of love, I began to listen and obey. I hope you will open your heart and listen too.

The Single Celibate

Single, Celibate and Dating

S ounds like a mouth full right? If you picked up this guide, then I am sure you can identify with these titles. This person is single, abstaining from sex, but still desires to date in hopes of finding a potential mate chosen by God. A mate that is equally yoked with them and has the same conviction to wait until marriage. To be single is one thing, but trying to date and wait for marriage before having sex is a completely different struggle. In your desire to remain abstinent, I am sure you are finding it hard to figure out what to do while you're single, right? You are trying to figure out how to exactly "wait" on God. Possibly even wondering if it is okay to even date at all. You are also unsure of how to date someone and not be physical while wondering what exactly is this "boundary" in dating that everyone talks about. How do I know? Because I had the same questions. You are probably also frustrated with dating because of the lack of prospects who are actually okay with waiting.

Whether you were told in church, or maybe a parent tried to persuade you, you have probably been told it is best to wait, but no one has actually told you how to do it. They may have told you just to pray and run from temptation. To run like Joseph and leave everything at the moment of temptation. Or maybe they told you to just control your flesh. Has that helped? Probably not. In this lifestyle, you need a step by step guide on what is okay and what's not okay. What to do while you're single, dating and how exactly to date. I can totally understand these questions, for I was there myself.

Trying to figure out exactly what to do can be extremely hard, and to say the least, frustrating beyond explanation. Wanting to find a mate is a normal desire, and honestly, wanting to have sex is one too. It's our natural instinct to want to be with others, and the world does everything possible to remind us that this instinct is natural. They feed on this natural need in every way possible. Whether to sell you a burger or to get you to buy a new fragrance, they use that desire in us to sell because they know how important it is for singles to find love and attention. We naturally want to have companionship. It is in our coding to want to be with someone, mate and one day start a family. Going back to the times when it was just God and Adam, we see this desire spring up naturally. Adam was with God. The Almighty. The Creator. The Main Man. The Completer. Yet, even he felt alone.

Genesis 2:20 NIV *"So the man gave names to all the livestock, the birds in the sky and all the wild animals. But for Adam, no suitable helper was found."*

Though Adam had everything at his disposal, even God, he still did not feel that anything was suitable for companionship other than another human. God saw this need and provided it. This story has always given me a peace about having the desire to want to be with someone. It reminded me it was totally okay that I desired to have a spouse. So many people try to make singles feel bad for wanting a mate. There is nothing wrong with you desiring to be with someone. It is natural. The issue comes in when you put that person or desire before God or when you are looking for a mate to complete you or fill a void. Only God can do that for you. That's when the problem comes in. Do not feel bad for wanting a mate. God has created us to want to be with others. It's okay. Seeing how God provided for Adam, I have learned that it is okay for us to desire to have a mate. God saw that need in Adam, and He provided it. God will provide the same for you at His will and in His own way. It is best for some to be married while others it may not. Trust God with your desires and trust that He will fill it the way He sees fit, and it will be perfect.

Beyond us desiring companionship, we want to attain this companionship in a way that honors God. This is a struggle for multiple reasons. For one, the world tells us that being sexual is natural and freeing. They praise sexual promiscuity and see it as abnormal to withhold this desire. Two, it is easier to get tempted today more than ever. Sex is everywhere! We are bombarded with sex and promiscuity daily. Not only that, it is easily attainable. Instagram, Facebook, Snapchat, you name it. You can access some form of sexual arousal without even trying. Three, it is easier to get in compromising situations due to the independent nature of our society. We go out alone; we live alone, and we go on dates alone. We go off to college during the prime hormonal years of our lives. There isn't the same responsibility of community as there was years ago. There is no accountability. Four, we don't see the big deal with waiting. We have been told not to do it, but have no idea why we shouldn't. We don't see the harm and feel we are just missing out on something everyone else is doing.

So as we struggle with our issues of being single, we then come to the issue of pulling someone else into this whirlwind of struggles and questions. We want to date. Now we have to not only to be in the dating world, but we have to find someone who has a relationship with God, and here is the hardest part; someone who also wants to wait until marriage before having sex. It's ironic. You would think that a person being a believer would automatically come with the belief to abstain from premarital sex. Wrong! I am sure you have come across this issue quite frequently. I know I have for myself many times. I have even dated pastors who were more tempting than the average believer. It's crazy.

So what do we do? Do we become nuns or monks and keep ourselves detached from the world? Do we decide to be celibate indefinitely and not even bother with trying to deal with the frustrations of dating? Or do we give up on doing things God's way and fall into the world's plan for dating and marriage? Well, to be honest, that is up to you. I cannot force you to do anything. Not even God can force you to do anything. But I am hoping in this guide I can give you hope in this area, and you continue with your decision to wait for marriage, despite the frustrations. I am hoping that you cannot only identify with the struggle but also identify with the hope and joy in doing it God's way.

I firmly believe that God knows our hearts, knows our struggles and knows we need His help to finish this race; pure, righteous and faithfully. He knows we cannot do this alone, and He has given us the tools needed to have victory in this area and all areas of our lives. I hope at the end of this guide you will be able to see that you can have victory in this area realizing it is possible to be *Single, Celibate, and Dating.*

1 Corinthians 10:13 NLT *"The temptations in your life are no different from what others experience. And God is faithful. He will not allow the temptation to be more than you can stand. When you are tempted, he will show you a way out so that you can endure."*

1 Corinthians 12:9 NLT *"Each time he said, "My grace is all you need. My power works best in weakness." So now I am glad to boast about my weaknesses so that the power of Christ can work through me."*

Isaiah 41: 10 NLT *"Don't be afraid, for I am with you. Don't be discouraged, for I am your God. I will strengthen you and help you. I will hold you up with my victorious right hand."*

Why Not Have Sex Before Marriage?

If you are currently celibate, you may already know why it's important not to have sex before marriage. Or maybe you don't know beyond the typical church answer, "Because it's wrong." I am unsure about you, but when I was in church that is all I heard. No one ever told me why not to have sex other than because God instructed us not to and that's it. It was ingrained in me that it was a sin, and you just don't do it! Well, I am sure for many, just like me, that was not enough for me, and it definitely didn't help me to remain pure. Not at all. I did everything but have sex and eventually I was bored and ended up having sex. All due to lack of information and understanding. We need more than just the biblical staple answer to help us to understand why God has instructed us to remain pure. When you understand why it helps you fight harder for your celibacy.

In this portion of the guide, I will go over why it's important to wait for marriage. If you want more details on this area, I suggest my book *Not Tonight: My Worth Is Far*

Above Rubies. I go into more detail about my story as well as why it's important to wait.

We Become One With Our Partner

Matthew 19:5-6 NLT *"And he said, 'This explains why a man leaves his father and mother and is joined to his wife, and the two are united into one. Since they are no longer two but one, let no one split apart what God has joined together."*

God reserved sex for marriage due to the nature of what occurs during sex. Marriage is very important to God and is a representation of the relationship between Christ and the church. Christ sacrificed for the church, loves the church and is one with the church. He desires the same for partners in marriage. He desires unity between the two and implements this desire during the consummation of marriage. He wants unity and oneness. When you have sex with someone, you have become one with their spirit. They become a part of you, and you are a part of them. This bond was meant to be made between a husband and wife, and they are seen as one under God. It was a bond intended to enhance marriage and have two partners come together not only in the physical realm but spiritual. This is a beautiful representation of our relationship with Christ and the beauty of marriage. What you have to realize is that Jesus is committed to us. He will never leave us. He will never forsake us. We experience something with Him that can never be broken. It is an intimate relationship that you can trust. The issue comes in when you create this bond with someone who doesn't have that same commitment to you. You have formed a bond with them, and there is no trust, no commitment and lack of oneness with your partner.

When this bond is broken, the hurt that occurs is unfathomable. If you have ever had sex with someone, and there wasn't any type of real commitment, you know this feeling. I am sure you remember the hurt and betrayal.

Think about it. Why is it so hard to let go of someone you've had sex with? Why does it take so long to get over them? Why do you find yourself thinking of them all day as if you are inseparable?

You feel that something special has been violated that was very important and intimate. You are absolutely right; it is important. But you experienced it with someone who isn't committed to you. They didn't make that commitment before God nor before you. God wants to protect this act within the bond of marriage because He understands the power of this oneness and the hurt that occurs when it is broken. He just wants to protect you. Everything God instructs us to do is out of love and Him wanting us to experience our best possible life. Trust what He instructs. He created sex, so I am sure He understands it far better than we do and knows when it's best to partake in it. That's the key to understanding God's commandments and instruction.

Another concern is when you have sex with your partner you take on each other's traits, personality, habits, and spiritual issues they may have. That's the most dangerous thing that can happen within this act, you becoming one with someone that is unequally yoked with you.

2 Corinthians 6:14 NIV *"Do not be unequally yoked with unbelievers. For what partnership has righteousness with lawlessness? Or what fellowship has light with darkness?"*

If you are unsure what it means to be equally yoked with someone, let me explain. A yoke is a tool used among farmers to bind animals together as they work in the fields. This binding of animals connects them with another, therefore, whatever one does it affects the other. When the word yoke is used in this context, it is exclaiming that when you form that link with your partner, who is not the same spiritually, it can affect you, and not for the good. The Bible exclaims that if you connect yourself with someone who is spiritually immoral, you become the same.

1st Corinthians 6:16 NIV *"Or do you not know that the one who joins himself to a prostitute is one body with her? For He says, "THE TWO SHALL BECOME ONE FLESH."*

This can truly hit hard when understanding how real this is; I know that for me it was. In other words, if you have sex with someone, and they have had multiple partners, you become one with that same spirit. If that partner is dealing with addictions, you will start having issues as well. If that partner is emotionally disturbed, you will find yourself feeling the same. Whatever is within them spiritually, will be within you as well. It's even scarier when you think of the different partners they have been with. You have no idea who they have been involved with sexually! It truly shows how serious and dangerous it is to have sex with someone, unequally yoked. You are opening your spirit to God knows what. I remember a guy I was involved with in the past that I had sex with. I remember that as we continued having sex, it seemed I started to crave things I didn't before. I had desires that I was unsure of where they came from and that were unhealthy and definitely ungodly. I soon realized these were issues he never dealt with as well, and I had become a part of that. God doesn't want that type of connection in your life.

When you get married, He wants you to be connected as one to someone who has a love for Him and on the same purpose driven life; equally yoked. Someone who will make you better.

He desires this for us because He understands how important it is to have a mate that is driven by the same purpose. A yoke that helps and not hinders your life. God has a plan for your life, and He only desires for things and people to be in your life that will help you get to that goal. His will is always to prosper you and help you grow into the will He has for your life. If there are people or things in your life that are preventing you from growth, then begin to examine your life. Detach yourself from them. Ask God to break the bond between you and that partner. He will do it. He did it for me.

He Wants You Free From Concern

1 Corinthians 7: 32-35 NASB *"But I want you to be free from concern. One who is unmarried is concerned about the things of the Lord, how he may please the Lord: but one who is married is concerned about the things of the world, how he may please his wife, and his interests are divided. The woman who is unmarried, and the virgin, is concerned about the things of the Lord, that she may be holy both in body and spirit, but one who is married is concerned about the things of the world, how she may please her husband. This I say for your own benefit; not to put a restraint upon you, but to promote what is appropriate and to secure undistracted devotion to the Lord."*

Understand that when Paul wrote this to the Church of Corinth, there were many undefiled acts occurring between members of the church and he was giving instruction because of their situation at hand. But with that, he gave vital instruction on marriage and being single, even in our present time. The part I want you to notice is how he exclaims that the person who is not married, the virgin, is concerned only with the things of the Lord.

When you are married, you naturally find yourself thinking of your partner throughout the day. You want to provide their every need, and they become a major concern for you. You have to provide, care for them and think about what's best for them physically, emotionally, mentally and spiritually. You are concerned for their livelihood and want the best for them always. When you are single, you aren't concerned with pleasing a mate; but only pleasing God. Does this mean you can't be married and be concerned of the Lord as well? No. Paul is trying to explain that those concerns are pulled in more than one direction now. You can't focus completely on God. It's harder. Ask any married person if they find it harder in their marriage to get time with God one on one? Add kids to the equation and that's even harder.

Now I am not by any means saying that those who are married aren't concerned about the Lord, but what I am saying is that their interest is of their spouse as well.

When we are single, our concerns should be of God and His purpose that He has for us. When we are involved with someone sexually, especially a corrupt person, they influence you. They influence your thoughts, decisions, and attitude.

I remember one particular guy I was involved with sexually. All I thought about was his desires and what he wanted from me and his life. I started to maneuver things in my life to fit his and tried to create my own will instead of accepting God's. I still loved God, but I noticed that my desire, my vigor for God, was dwindling and was slowly becoming minute. My desires had turned to this man. God doesn't want that for us. He wants you to love him; concerned only with Him and His will. He wants your time of singleness to be a time to have a relationship with Him with your undivided attention. This is why God sees marriage and singleness as a blessing.

1 Corinthians MSG 7:7 *"Sometimes I wish everyone were single like me—a simpler life in many ways! But celibacy is not for everyone any more than marriage is. God gives the gift of the single life to some, the gift of the married life to others."*

Ecclesiastes 3:1 NIV *"There is a time for everything and a season for every activity under the heavens..."*

He Doesn't Want You To Be A Slave

1ˢᵗ Corinthians 6:18 KJV *"18 Flee from sexual immorality. All other sins a man commits are outside his body, but he who sins sexually sins against his own body."*

Every time you sin against God you are not only hurting your flesh but also your spirit.

John 8:34 KJV *"Verily, truly I tell you. Everyone who sins is a slave to sin."*

The world gives you the perception that you are independent, and you set the rules for yourself and life, especially when it comes to sex. They show you the riveting part of sex, being able to share such an intimate moment with someone and be sexually free. But in reality, you are subjecting yourself to be a slave, a slave to sin. The enemy will try to deceive you into thinking that you are free when you are actually binding yourself to a sin that is hard to escape. Don't be deceived, sex outside of marriage is not freedom, it is enslavement.

I remember hearing a pastor go over the importance of not having sex before marriage. He brought up that God did not create our bodies to have sex and then stop. That really shocked me. I thought to myself, "So since I have had sex before there is no way for me to practice celibacy?" Then I realized what he truly meant. He was trying to show us that it's better not to start having sex until you are married because your body will crave it. Your body will expect it. It is in our nature to desire things we have had before.

Think about it. You didn't desire certain things until you first tried it. If you had never tried it, you wouldn't crave it because you had never experienced before. Just as normal things in your life you crave, there are things you didn't crave until after you experienced it. Sex is the same way. Though you do crave it, it doesn't have as much power over you because you haven't actually had it. But when you do have it, it is hard to stop, but not impossible.

If you have had sex before and are trying to go into the life of celibacy, you know exactly what I am talking about. It's hard! Your body will react to things that you didn't even expect it to. As if it has its own mind. You will find your mind searching for a potential past partner just to get a release from the tension. It's tough. But it is not impossible!

There are certain things you have to do to prevent the temptation and also to prevent you from falling to an act that can have control over you. God doesn't want that for us. He wants us to have control over our bodies, not our bodies have control over us. Be free.

He Wants To Prevent You From Unnecessary Heartache

God loves us very much. He wants the best for you and He, in every way possible, tries to prevent you from unnecessary heartache. Does that mean you will never go through anything? No. As Christians, we will suffer as

Christ did and we will also be exalted as Christ was as well. But some things we experience can be prevented if we follow and are patient in God's will. Having sex with your partner before marriage is opening yourself up for possible heartache if:

- You are unequally yoked
- There is no commitment
- There are no intentions of marriage

The bond of sex is very strong, and He doesn't want you to experience breaking that bond with someone who doesn't care for you and has no intentions of marrying you. That is the risk you are taking. I know we want to be loved, and we want to have that commitment, but sometimes you have to watch it and not let it control you to the point that you are making bad decisions for your life. I have been there. I have made some decisions that put me through heartache that was very unnecessary. All because of the need of wanting companionship. Dating guys I knew weren't good for me. Staying in relationships knowing they weren't the one. Moving too fast off of the phase of infatuation.

When you form that bond, it is something that is hard to break and takes a long process. Just as it took you time to fall in love with them, it will also take you time to fall out of love and to break that bond. Be strong. Think of your well-being. Wait until the right time. Am I saying you will never have any heartache when you are involved with your partner sexually in marriage? No. No relationship is perfect. But you all are committed to each other and to

God. You have made a commitment before God and a covenant with each other. Ensure to make that commitment with someone who doesn't take that covenant lightly. Someone who will do anything to keep you all together and not give up on the importance of keeping you all as one under God. Someone who truly believes in, "…till death do us part."

It Affects Your Body In Ways You Can't Control

"God did not create sex for us to start and then stop"-Anonymous.

I will never forget when I heard this quote. I was listening to a sermon on a bible app and was truly intrigued by this comment. Now someone may hear this comment and begin to think, "See, even God doesn't think I should stop having sex since I've started." But that is definitely not what that pastor was trying to emphasize in this statement. When I first heard it, I immediately thought about how much harder it was for me to stop having sex after I started. You probably can remember yourself as well. Do you remember how much easier it was to say no to sex when you hadn't experienced it yet? I do. It wasn't as hard to fight the urge because I hadn't experienced it yet. It was easy for me to tell a guy no or push him away. However, after I experienced sex, it was ten times harder to say no. It was as if my body craved for it and it had to be satisfied some way. After I had heard this statement, I decided to look more into this to see what actually happens to our bodies when we have sex. What is going on that even when the person hurts you; you crave them? Why is it so hard to resist the urge even when you have a huge list of reasons on why not to do it? Why do you find yourself craving it even when it isn't on your mind? Does it sometimes feel like an addiction? Well, the reality is when you are having sex the same "high" that people get from drugs happens during sex. When you have sex, you have a release of something called *dopamine*. This is a neurotransmitter that activates the reward part of your brain. See what Dr. Timothy Fong says about sex and the brain in a Health Article entitled, *8 Ways Sex Affects Your Brain*.

"Taking cocaine and having sex don't feel exactly the same, but they do involve the same brain regions as well as different regions of the brain," says Timothy Fong, MD

He compares it to the same chemical reaction that happens during drug usage. The article even goes on to explain that sex can be an anti-depressant, pain reliever as well as stress reliever. Wow, sex is doing a lot for us. But it was all intended to do so with our spouses. To enjoy it fully without the hurt of withdrawal, betrayal or lack of commitment. The more I read about the physiological effects of sex it was another reminder to trust God's direction. He knows what he's talking about! He knew everything that would happen when we started to have sex, and He wanted to reserve this gift for marriage. He understood the amazing effects it could have on our bodies and wanted us to experience it with our spouse. We truly have to start listening to our Father more. He created us. He knows what our bodies are capable of and gives us direction based on this knowledge.

The Unknown

Ephesians 5:31 *"For this reason a man shall leave his father and mother and be joined to his wife, and the two shall become one flesh. This is a great mystery, but I speak concerning Christ and the church. NKJV"*

The Bible brings up marriage quite a bit, and this is one of the scriptures that I really love. When it discusses the husband and wife becoming one flesh it reminded me of the importance of having a mate equally yoked because you are becoming one with them. One. I don't know about you, but I don't want to become one with just anyone. But what really stuck out to me is the portion that discusses it being, "...a great mystery." God has done and continues to do things that we don't understand and probably never will. There are things that are beyond our understanding and may stay misunderstood until we meet the Father. The Bible discusses our lack of knowledge compared to God's knowledge.

Isaiah 55: 8-9 *"For my thoughts are not your thoughts, neither are your ways my ways. As the heavens are higher than your ways and my thoughts than your thoughts. (NIV)"*

God's ways and thoughts are unfathomable to us, and we can't even begin to try and understand Him. Though sometimes we try to attempt to. So I know what you're thinking, "Chloe, why are you saying all of this?" I am bringing this up because, honestly, there are some things about sex that we will never understand. There are some things we will never be able to explain about sex and the body nor about sex and the spirit. I can try my best to inform you about the dangers of sex before marriage, but there are some things I am just simply not aware of because I am not God.

This is important to note. We have to learn to trust God's instruction and not play with His design. We have to obey him, even when we don't understand it. There are things that I know I have felt for someone, and I am sure you have as well, that cannot be explained. I couldn't figure out why I still wanted to go back to them after they had hurt me. I couldn't figure out why I could still feel them, even when they were not there. I didn't understand why I would yearn for them even when they weren't on my mind. I have been there, and I am sure you have too. It is inconceivable to understand totally what happens and another reason why we just need to listen to God. It's just like when you were a child. Your parents probably told you not to do a lot of things. Some of them you immediately understood why you shouldn't do it and others you didn't quite get so quickly. You either were like me and terrified to do what my parents told me not to do, or either you were the rebellious type and tried it anyways. Either way, you somehow found out why they forewarned you not to engage in certain things.

Whether from your own personal experience or maturity, you eventually realized why they said it and realized they were only trying to protect you. They wanted the best for you. That is the same way God feels about us. God loves you a lot. Though it may seem He is trying to prevent you from having "fun," He is only trying to protect you. Though you may not completely understand why He is telling you to wait, just trust Him. He loves His children and only wants to protect you, not cause harm to you. Trust in His guidance.

Distraction In Dating

You meet a great person and of course, you want to get to know them and see if they're someone you could see as a potential mate. What do you do to see if they are the right one? I am sure you do what everyone does. Go out on a couple of dates to see their personality. Talk for a while to see who they are, their goals and their aspirations. You want to get to know the ins and outs of the person so you can make sure you are making the right choice. Totally understandable. There are a lot of things we should pay attention to and ask about when dating. I talk more about this in my book *Single to Married*. We all want to make sure we are dating someone we could be with long term. I mean that's the whole reason for dating. So I am sure if there was anything that could distract you from seeing who they are, you would want to remove it right?

Let's say if the entire time you are getting to know someone you found out later they'd been lying to you. Every word they said was to get you distracted into thinking they were honest, sweet and loyal. You would be pretty upset right? Wondering the entire time why they tried to deceive you. Well, did you know that when you have sex with someone that bond can be a blinder? A blinder that could keep you from seeing the truth. Well, that's exactly what happens. When we have sex with someone we are distracted by the connection we have with them, and we see them as someone who we will be with forever. We fall in love. You have already placed in your body, spirit and mind that they are your spouse, and you will do anything to keep that connection, including ignoring the signs that they may not be right for you.

It disables your ability to pay attention to who a person truly is because you are in love with the connection. You forget to discuss those important things like long term goals, family, and ambitions. Even if you do discuss it, you don't pay attention to those goals that you all disagree with.

Let's say for instance you want to be a stay at home wife and mother one day. In the beginning, your partner informs you that they will never be okay with that. Well, you hear this but you bring up to him you will still work some but just want to be at home the majority of the time. Maybe his response sounds possibly open to your idea but in the end, he tells you that isn't something he desires. Because you are involved with him sexually, and possibly in love, you can't imagine letting him go. You hear that it isn't a desire, but you continue dating him forgetting that he doesn't have the same ultimate goal. Several months later while dating the topic comes up again, and he still feels the same way; he doesn't want a stay at home wife/mother. You still desire this, and it causes a major argument and possibly even a breakup. But why are you surprised? This was brought up at the beginning of the relationship. This is nothing new. You all cannot agree on this, and you all end up going your separate ways. All of this hurt could have been avoided if you had paid attention to who they were and what they truly want in life. But that connection distracted you.

Even if you both possibly have the same long term goals, maybe there are some red flags popping up that you can't deal with in a relationship. Maybe you notice they go drinking three days a week, and it seems it's becoming an addiction. Maybe you notice they go through a pack of cigarettes a day and it's draining their pocket and health. Maybe you notice that they go from job to job within months and don't seem too stable. Well, even when you see behaviors that are red flags, you will do everything possible to keep the relationship going because you can't imagine losing them.

When you keep that disconnect physically, and spiritually, you are able to pay attention to who they are and make a logical decision on whether it is a relationship you should continue with or not. Notice I said "logical" decision. You will be able to think with your mind and not your feelings. You are able to leave the relationship without it making a detrimental hit to your heart.

Wait to have sex with your partner until they are your spouse. Anytime you take a step as if they are your spouse, and you aren't even sure who they are; you are telling yourself they are the one and will do anything to fight for it. But God intended that fight for marriage. You have made that bond before God, and you are willing to do anything to fight for it to keep that covenant in tack. Which is normal and encouraged in a marriage. But when they aren't your spouse, you may be fighting for a connection that should have never been made. Wait. Save such an intimate relationship for an intimate covenant; marriage.

Reflection

You may have heard something new in this section in regards as to why you should wait, or you may have known them all. That's great! Beyond the reasons for why you should not have sex before marriage, you truly should have reasons individually for why you want to wait. A big part of being able to remain faithful in your decision is making a personal commitment to God. I want you to take a journal out or a sheet of paper. On that paper, I want you to write down the reasons you are waiting for marriage to have sex. It could be something like, "I want to honor God," or "I don't want to do anything that will weaken my relationship with God." Whatever the reasons, write them down. Write down at least ten reasons why you want to wait. After doing that, I want you to place it somewhere you will always see it. Another good practice is to place it in your wallet or purse. Have it handy so that anytime you feel yourself getting frustrated, or tempted to change your mind, you can have it readily available to read and be reminded of your promise to God and yourself.

The Do's & Don'ts of the
Single & Celibate

O n this journey of singleness and celibacy, it can sometimes become confusing as to what exactly we are supposed to do as we wait on a potential spouse. Or what to do if you have no desire to become a potential spouse and just want to be able to remain abstinent indefinitely. No matter the category that you fall into, there are certain things that we should avoid; as well as some things we should actively practice to remain pure in mind, heart, spirit, and soul.

As I stated before, and I am sure you have realized yourself; sex is everywhere. It's sometimes hard to keep it off of our minds no matter how much we try to refrain from thinking about it. We can read scriptures, watch sermons, keep our minds on things righteous and true, not watch certain movies, everything we can think of to keep our minds pure. Yet right when you walk out of your moment of purity, you see a sex filled commercial or hear someone discussing their previous night's rendezvous. No matter how hard we try, it is slapped in our faces every chance the world gets. The more we see it and unconsciously think about it, it can become frustrating, and we find ourselves needing some form of release to be able to deal with it. The frustrations can become hard to deal with, and you start to feel as if it's pointless to try and wait. So you try to find some form of release. Some people deal with their frustrations by going to work out or maybe focusing their energy on a particular hobby. To each their own. Though everyone deals with these frustrations in different ways, there are some ways that are unhealthy and sinful that we should not engage in personally. I am going to hit on some touchy topics throughout this section so be prepared. I am going to go over the taboo subjects that many will not discuss.

Please know that I am not in any way trying to judge you as a celibate believer. I am purely going over this to help you. I have been here and have slipped up many times. I did things that I thought were okay, as long as I didn't actually "have sex." I was totally wrong, and I fell into sin ignorantly. I didn't know it was wrong for multiple reasons, and I am hoping to keep you from making the same mistakes. The enemy loves to deceive us and make us think that certain things we are doing in life are harmless. That's how he gets us enslaved to sin.

2 Corinthians 11:3 *"But I am afraid that just as Eve was deceived by the serpent's cunning, your minds may somehow be led astray from your sincere and pure devotion to Christ(NIV)."*

He is great at it. The bible even discusses how he even disguises himself as the light. He will do anything to make you think certain things are innocent and harmless to your goal of righteousness. He knows if he can deceive you with little things that eventually you will become numb to the big things. He knows how we function. You have to remember that the enemy comes to kill, steal and destroy. He is doing everything possible to ensure you fail. That's why it's so important that we are always armored to fight the good fight of faith.

Ephesians 6:11-20 *"Put on the full armor of God, so that you can take your stand against the devil's schemes. 12 For our struggle is not against flesh and blood, but against the rulers, against the authorities, against the powers of this dark world and against the spiritual forces of evil in the heavenly realms. 13 Therefore put on the full armor of God, so that when the day of evil comes, you may be able to stand your ground, and after you have done everything, to stand. 14 Stand firm then, with the belt of truth buckled around your waist, with the breastplate of righteousness in place, 15 and with your feet fitted with the readiness that comes from the gospel of peace. 16 In addition to all this, take up the shield of faith, with which you can extinguish all the flaming arrows of the evil one. 17 Take the helmet of salvation and the sword of the Spirit, which is the word of God. 18 And pray in the Spirit on all occasions with all kinds of prayers and requests. With this in mind, be alert and always keep on praying for all the Lord's people. 19 Pray also for me, that whenever I speak, words may be* *given me so that I will fearlessly make known the mystery of the gospel, 20 for which I am an ambassador in chains. Pray that I may declare it fearlessly, as I should(NIV)."*

You must have a plan. You have to be prepared in every way possible. You wouldn't go to war without getting your armor, right? Well did you know you are in a war every day of your life? You are. Put on your armor. One way to start is by being aware of what is wrong and right in your wait.

The best way to know if something you are doing is wrong; pay attention to your spirit. Even when things are not written out plainly in the Word, your spirit will always give you a tug that gives you an uneasiness. Think about the times in your past that you were about to engage in something wrong, or maybe already in the act, do you remember that moment that you just didn't feel right? That moment that makes you feel, "Something is wrong with what I'm doing." We all have felt it. If you are saved and have the holy spirit residing in you, which you do, you will always have that tug at your spirit. It never goes away. God will always convict us in wrong actions because He is trying to save us. Everything he does is to help us. He is only helping you with that tug of uneasiness. You can decide to follow the conviction or decide to ignore it and go ahead with your actions. Regardless, know that every action has a consequence. If you feel you are not aware of this tug of conviction, ask God to make you more sensitive to the spirit. He will do this for you. Just ask.

James 1:5 NIV *"If any of you lacks wisdom, you should ask God, who gives generously to all without finding fault, and it will be given to you."*

The Do's and Don'ts

Part I

Don't Engage in These Activities

Don't Engage in "Self-Pleasure."

Taboo subject, right? It isn't discussed in the bible and we definitely never hear about it in the church. No one discusses it, yet, many believers fall into this sin frequently; masturbation. This is an easy thing to fall into because many think that it's okay because you aren't actually having sex with someone, and it is even sometimes condoned to alleviate sexual tension. Trust me; I thought the same thing. You probably feel that it's okay because at least you aren't having sex with someone right? You are just trying to find a way to deal with the frustration. I totally get it.

The more I grew in my faith; I felt the Holy Spirit always tugging at my heart about this issue. I had to realize that just because something is not laid out blatantly in the bible does not mean it is right. I am sure there are things you have done that you are unsure if it's right or wrong sometimes. Yet, there is something within us that gives us an uneasy feeling to quickly guide us in the right direction. Sometimes we go with the feeling; sometimes we don't. One day while reading the Word, I ran across a scripture that truly opened my mind to the expectations of God.

Romans 14:22-23 NLT *"You may believe there's nothing wrong with what you are doing, but keep it between yourself and God. Blessed are those who don't feel guilty for doing something they have decided is right. [23] But if you have doubts about whether or not you should eat something, you are sinning if you go ahead and do it. For you are not following your convictions. If you do anything you believe is not right, you are sinning."*

If you notice, the scripture states by you simply not following your convictions; you are sinning. Wow. When I saw this, I was seriously in awe. It reminded me as well that God truly does cover everything in our lives. See, God knows us very well. He knew that there was no way possible for him to lay out every single thing we could possibly do wrong because honestly it's a lot. I truly feel He placed this scripture here to cover it all. Whether or not it is laid out plainly in the Bible, God has given us the Holy Spirit to guide us in our walk. I quickly realized that self-pleasure was wrong, and it wasn't helping me in my celibacy walk at all. How? Let me show you.

Here are some reasons why:

- **Anything outside of God's order is a sin.** God ordained for sex to be shared in the union of marriage. Not alone. Sex brings you closer to your partner while self-pleasure simply brings you closer to yourself. How so? You start to get to a place where you don't need someone else to please you. You result to depending on yourself for intimacy, and it's purely sexual. Simply to satisfy your needs of the flesh. One thing I have learned about God is that He desires for us to need each other and commune with each other. To please and show love to one another. When you do it for yourself, you are taking away your partner's ability to show their love for you through intimacy. The enemy knows this and encourages us to do things that help us commune with ourselves and rely on ourselves, instead of others. Out of God's order.

- **We have to have lustful thoughts to engage in self-pleasure.** God instructs us not to lust after anything, and He also instructs us to think on things that are good, lovely, pure, righteous and of good report. Are your thoughts enhancing any of these things?

   Philippians 4:8 NIV *"Finally, brothers and sisters, whatever is true, whatever is noble, whatever is right, whatever is pure, whatever is lovely, whatever is admirable—if anything is excellent or praiseworthy—think about such things."*

- **You will eventually become numb to the act and want more.** The self-pleasure won't satisfy your hunger, and after a while, you will find yourself pursuing other things to fulfill the urge. The flesh is never satisfied. Think about drug addicts. It always begins with a small amount of substance, but eventually they want more, and that is most generally what causes the overdose. The same thing happens with sex. The more you are intimate with yourself you eventually want more to satisfy the urge. You will want the real thing. It will no longer be a fantasy, but your reality.

- **You will relate sex to a physical act more than a spiritual connection to a partner.** Sex will become more of an act you enjoy to partake in for sexual pleasure instead of connection with your partner. Does God want you to enjoy sex? Of course. But does He only want you to focus on the act and not your partner? No. He wants you all to enjoy each other and focus on each other. As my fiance and I were in counseling we were told that during sex you should focus on pleasing the other. That totally made sense to me. If each person is focused on the other, then everyone is taken care of. It was also a reminder that sex is about communing with your partner and not focused on self.

1 Corinthians 7: 2-6 MSG *"The marriage bed must be a place of mutuality—the husband seeking to satisfy his wife, the wife seeking to satisfy her husband. Marriage is not a place to "stand up for your rights." Marriage is a decision to serve the other, whether in bed or out."*

- **You will have a lack of patience with your partner sexually.** Since you have been engaging in self-pleasure, you know exactly how you want things and know how to get yourself there quickly. Now, for some, they feel this is a great thing because then you know what you like and can tell your partner. You see many magazines and books actually encouraging us to do it. But the Bible reminds us, *"Do not conform to the pattern of this world, but be transformed by the renewing of your mind. Then you will be able **to** test and approve what God's will is—his good, pleasing and perfect will (**Romans 12:2 NIV**)."*

The issue with this advice is the missing purpose God has for sex. When you are with your partner, you have to allow your partner to get to know you physically. You learn together and make your own "love" with each other. It's truly a beautiful thing God has created. But you take that away when you figure it out for yourself, and you lose patience with your partner. Why? Because you already know what you like and become frustrated that your partner is taking a bit longer. Wait to learn your body with your partner. Learn each other. You will be glad you waited to explore and find each other's love together. That's what God intended for us, and when it's done right, it's beautiful.

Don't convince yourself to do it "Just this one time."

You will find yourself frustrated a lot in this daily walk, and the enemy will do everything he can do to get you to fall. He will work with your mind as much as possible to get you to fall into the trap of having sex. I remember even thinking that if I could just have sex one time, then I would be fine, and I at least was able to see what it was like. Wrong! Don't let the enemy get in your mind that it is a harmless act that you can stop as easily as you started. As you date, you will find yourself in positions of thinking you may want to try this out even though you know it is wrong. I am telling you from experience, once you start, it is very hard to go back. Is it impossible? No. But it definitely makes the task a bit harder. Remain faithful in your walk. Do not let the enemy play with your mind. It's just like if you are on a diet and trying to avoid sweets. You don't ask for a piece of cake and then only eat half of it right? It's too hard. You've tasted the chocolate, the moist cake, and you want more! Same way with sex. Don't try to engage in it once and think you will not go back or want to continue to indulge in it. You are only fooling yourself. It is better to stay away from the dessert!

Do not watch Pornography

You may already know that you shouldn't watch pornography, or you possibly didn't see it as an issue. Some people feel they can watch pornography, and it causes no harm to them nor anyone else. Once again, this is a deception from the enemy. Scripture informs us to watch what we set our eyes upon as well as advises us not to lust after others.

Psalms 101:3 ESV *"I will not set before my eyes anything that is worthless. I hate the work of those who fall away; it shall not cling to me."*

Matthew 5:28 ESV *"But I say to you that everyone who looks at a woman (or man) with lustful intent has already committed adultery with her in his heart.*

We are focusing on something immoral, and it affects our thoughts. When we see pornography, it gets into our thoughts and eventually our dreams. When it gets into our dreams, we begin to think about this incessantly and eventually want to do it. It becomes who we are. We constantly think about it, and we eventually do what we can to pursue it. The thought becomes an action; action becomes a habit, and the habit leads to life or death. The desire becomes a part of who you are and you become that desire.

Proverbs 23:7 AMP *"For as he thinks in his heart, so is he."*

I want to share a story with you just to give you an idea of how powerful pornography can be to the mind.

When I was in school, I took some counseling classes. One particular class I took was *Child Sexual Abuse.* Why did I take this class? I have no idea, but I did. Lord knows why?! I honestly heard some horrific stories in that class, but I learned a lot. One story that stuck in my mind was a young man who used to molest his two cousins, a little girl, and boy. Our teacher would have predators come to the class to help us understand the psychology behind what they were doing. This predator really stuck out to me. When they discussed the story behind what started the molestation against their cousins, it really shocked me. The predator informed us that they used to watch porn incessantly and would masturbate. Eventually, they were tired of masturbating and wanted to feel the real thing. Well, they had small cousins that they watched every day as their parents were at work. One day they decided to partake in what they saw on TV with their younger cousins. Horrific right? I know. It was for me as well. I truly think it was meant for me to hear that story. It stuck in my mind how serious and evil pornography is for to the mind and spirit. Pornography feeds others sexual addictions such as molestation, rape and more.

Everything has a spirit behind it. Everything. Now if we know anything, pornography is definitely not of God. Therefore, it will only produce things that are not of God as well. What will you produce by watching porn? I promise you it will not be something of God.

Do not condemn yourself for mishaps and mistakes

Romans 3:12 NLT "For everyone has sinned; we all fall short of God's glorious standard."

I pray that you don't make mistakes, but the truth of the matter is, you will. We are all imperfect human beings and God knew this; that's why He sent us Jesus Christ. You may slip up into one of these categories that I talked about above. That is okay. Ask for forgiveness. Repent. Adjust. Move forward. God didn't give us grace and mercy for nothing. He knew we would need His grace. He knew we would need His mercy. Now he didn't give it to us to continue in sin. He gave us the grace to correct our behavior.

Romans 6:1-2 *"What shall we say, then? Shall we go on sinning so that grace may increase? ² By no means! We are those who have died to sin; how can we live in it any longer (NIV)?"*

He knew we would need Jesus Christ. God is a God of conviction, not condemnation. The enemy will try and get you to feel bad about your mistakes in your walk. He will even try to convince you that there is no point in moving forward and trying to remain abstinent because it's impossible. It is not impossible. Just keep moving forward. God has already forgiven you. He will continue to give you the strength you need. He is not mad at you. He loves you and adores you. He is walking right beside you. The key is to remember that you can always call on God to give you strength where you are weak. Right now you know what your weaknesses are. You know if you have engaged in anything I have discussed above. Talk to God and ask Him to give you strength where you are struggling. He will help you. That's a promise.

Reflection

Write down some of the things you have possibly done in your past that you need forgiveness and freedom from. Talk to God about your struggles and ask Him to help you in your walk. Tell Him your weaknesses.

Tell Him how much you need Him. After you write them down, write a plan of how you will refrain from engaging in the acts I mentioned above, or any sexual acts that you know you've had conviction about from God. Keep this plan with you or memorize it. Afterward, pray and ask God to show you how to do this with Him. I will start the prayer for you. You can personalize it as needed.

"God, thank you for loving me and always being here when I need you. God, your Word says that I can cast my cares on you, and you will sustain me. That you lend an ear to your righteous child. Lord, I pray you lend an ear to your righteous child and help me in this walk. God, I am struggling. I need your help. My body craves for things that are not of you and out of order. God help me to think purely. God help me keep myself out of situations that I know are not of you. Lord take the desires from me that are not of you and replace them with your desires, thoughts and will. Forgive me of my sins. I pray for your grace and mercy..."

The Do's and Don'ts

Part II

Engage in These Activities

Have the right intentions for waiting.

Jeremiah 17:10 *"I the Lord search the heart and examine the mind, so reward each person according to their conduct, according to what their deeds deserve(NIV)."*

Waiting for marriage is a great decision to make for yourself physically, mentally and spiritually. I am sure you may have possibly been through some past hurts, or possibly just experienced how hurtful it can be from the outside perspective of a friend. Maybe that situation hit you to the core, and you want something to change? Or maybe you've never had sex and just need to know how to continue waiting in today's world. Whatever reason may have triggered you to wait, ensure that it is the right reason. When I say this, I am referring to your motives behind why you are deciding to wait. I remember doing a speaking event for a young girls group at a university in my hometown. One of the questions I asked them is, "Why are you waiting?". Some answered that they were waiting for their husband while others said they were waiting to be able to save it for that one special person. I then asked them, "What if you never get married?" Many of them stopped and didn't know what to say. I began to discuss with them that many women tend to wait on that potential spouse, which is a great goal, but should we not be waiting as a sacrifice and obedience to God? If not, your intentions are wrong. Everything we do should be for the glory of God and to live righteously. You will know if your intentions are right when you think of the answer to my question, "What if you were never to marry? Then what?". I have had some answer that if they didn't marry they would not be able to wait. While others said, they didn't see the point in waiting if they weren't ever going to give it to that special person.

Whatever we do, we should be focused on God, not on what we can gain from our sacrifice. Sad to say, but many people have the wrong intentions for why they are waiting, and this is usually why they aren't receiving what they have asked of God. You have to keep in mind that God knows our hearts. He searches us and sees the true intentions of everything we do. If He sees the intentions are wrong, He will not grant us what we ask. Stop and truly think about why you are deciding to wait. Are you doing it for man, or are you doing it for God? If your intentions are wrong, you will have a hard time staying committed to your decision.

James 4:3 *"When you ask, you do not receive, because you ask with wrong motives, that you may spend what you get on your pleasures(NIV)."*

Have a plan for times of weakness.

Moments of weakness will come. It is inevitable. We are in the flesh, and we will find ourselves having urges or in situations that require us to remain strong and make the wrong or right choice. In those times, it's much harder to stick to your decision because your emotions take over your logical thinking. The only thing you will pay attention to in that situation is your body. To prevent this, always have a plan. Without a plan, you are bound to fail. Write down things you can do to prevent yourself from falling into temptation. You know your triggers. You know when it's easiest for you to fall into temptation. Think back to the times you have fallen, track back to how you got there and figure out a plan that works for you.

For instance, if you know watching movies with sexual innuendos will make your imagination run wild, then possibly commit to not watching them. Or maybe you can't handle listening to vulgar music. Vow to stop listening to music that emphasizes exactly what you are trying not to do. For me, I know that music is a sensitive thing for me. When songs have sexual lyrics, it seeps into my mind, and I begin to imagine things or reminisce on my past. Since I know this about myself, I have decided not to listen to certain types of music. I know that's really extreme for many, but I personally made that decision years ago and have grown to love the peace and quiet at home and in my car. You don't have to be this extreme, but just find out what works best for you.

This is the thing. You will have to make some decisions that seem odd to those around you. But understand this, what is seen as right by God is seen as foreign to the world. Be prepared for others to think what you are doing is crazy. I've been there. But you are not trying to please man; only God. Contemplate on what plan you will have when you enter into a tough situation or things you can do to prevent even getting in the situation.

Here are just a few suggestions, but also add your personal ones. Also, some of these suggestions may not affect you at all. Some people can watch certain movies or read certain books, and it doesn't affect them one bit. So ensure to make a list of the things that hit home for you.

- I won't watch movies that are above a PG-13 rating.
- I won't listen to music that has explicit sexual lyrics.
- I won't read sensual novels.
- I won't entertain sexual conversations with potential partners.
- I won't use my personal computer for anything beyond educational and positive, pure social means.
- I won't spend the night with a potential partner no matter the situation.
- I won't think of my potential partner in a sexual way intentionally.
- I won't entertain a relationship with someone who doesn't value waiting.

- I won't give time to those who aren't in agreement with my decision.
- I won't engage in foreplay with my partner.
- I will have an accountability partner to ensure I stay on track.

Be conscious of who you decide to date.

In your decision to wait, you will have to be with someone who will work with you to wait for marriage. If one is weak, it may cause weakness for the other and vice versa. It's important to realize you all are working as a team. You have to stay focused on the goal you both have set to wait, and be focused and firm about your decision. If you all aren't working together and on the same mindset, you will continuously run into issues. But if you both are on the same page, you will be a perfect help to each other.

You want to ensure you all are like-minded. When I say this, I am referring to their values, goals, love for God and beliefs. If you are dating someone who doesn't agree with your decision, you are setting yourself up for failure. Now some people feel that you shouldn't judge others based off of their level of faith and shouldn't disregard them. Understand there is a difference with fellowship with others and having an intimate bond with someone. You are not disregarding them in a judgmental way. You want to ensure that if you are going to date, they will be there as a help and not a hindrance in your walk. You will have times that you are weak and want to be physical with your partner. You need someone who will not only stop you in your tracks but remind you of your promise to God. Also, when you have someone on the same page, you are able to work together as a team to remain celibate. You both will ensure not to put each other in situations that could lead to undesirable consequences.

Make sure they not only will respect your decision to be celibate, but they also agree with your beliefs and have the same goal as well. While I was dating, I would come across potential partners who respected my decision, but they didn't necessarily agree or understand my decision. I would tell them about my desires, and they would respond, "I respect that," or "I hear you." But that doesn't tell you anything about their beliefs on waiting. Ask questions. Dig deep to see if you all are on common ground. This caused issues later that taught me the importance of being equally yoked. I fell into sin quickly, because when I was weak, they were not strong. We were both weak in the situation, and we both fell. You want someone who can pick you up. Someone who can be your strength when you are weak.

Ecclesiastes 4:10 *"If either of them falls down, one can help the other up. But pity anyone who falls and has no one to help them up."*

Stay Prayerful

Zechariah 4:6 KJV *"Then he answered and spoke unto me, saying, "This is the word of the LORD unto Zerubbabel, saying, 'Not by might nor by power, but by My Spirit,' saith the LORD of hosts."*

Praying is an essential part of staying strong in your walk. We cannot do this alone. We simply cannot. We need God's help, and we will fail if we try to attempt doing it without Him. I have attempted many times to walk with my own plans and power, and it has failed me every time. We need constant communication and connection with our divine source to be able to fight temptation and remain pure. When you pray to God, He hears you each and every single time.

During this time, God strengthens you and communes with you. He gives you wisdom, power and increased desire to do His will. Don't forsake this important part of your walk with Christ. He wants an intimate relationship with you and the more intimate the relationship, the better. Remember that prayer is not done one way. Think of prayer as a simple conversation with God. Go to Him about your weakness.

Ask Him to give you wisdom in this area and to help you remain faithful to your promise. He will answer. He will always help you. God wants you to be successful in this walk as much as you do. He will give you everything you need to do so.

Philippians 2:13 NLT *"For God is working in you, giving you the desire and the power to do what pleases him."*

Read Your Bible Consistently

Joshua 1:8 NLT *"Study this Book of Instruction continually. Meditate on it day and night so you will be sure to obey everything written in it. Only then will you prosper and succeed in all you do."*

In order for you to walk righteously, you have to know God's word and what He requires of us to do so. If you don't know His Word, how do you expect to know what pleases Him? I am not implying if you don't memorize the Bible front to back you aren't sufficient enough. I haven't done this myself. But what I am implying is the importance of reading the Word so you can know it and so you can keep it fresh in your mind. When I step away from God's word, I find myself slipping into sin because His Word wasn't fresh on my mind. I wasn't meditating on it. Therefore, it wasn't in my heart.

The more you read the Word, the more it becomes a part of who you are. You will naturally walk in His Word because it has become a part of your daily thought process, desires, and speech. Walking according to His word will become natural for you. It is also important because you need it to combat the enemy. Anytime the enemy tried to attack Jesus he immediately responded back to Him with scripture. He understood the power in God's word. How can you combat the enemy's lies if you don't know the truth? It may be difficult for some of us to open up a Bible and simply begin to read. Understandable. Luckily, this generation has made it easier for us to read His word. If you don't have your own Bible handy, then you can possibly download an App. For me personally, I downloaded an app and I enjoy reading devotionals on particular topics. That way I am reading scriptures that are in line with my current situation. Download an App and search a title such as Temptation, Celibacy or Faith! Topic devotionals are great! Find your own way of meditating on the Word.

Whether downloading an app, reading a scripture a day, or listening to the Word online, find something that will refresh your mind of God's Word.

Be mindful of your thoughts.

"An Idle Mind is the Devils Playground."

I am sure you have heard this quote above before at some point in your life. I never knew how true this was until my later years. Usually, when I found myself focusing on things that were not of God, I was simply bored. Have you ever noticed the first place your mind reverts to when you are bored? I started to realize how important it was to be intentional with my thinking and ensure to refocus them on things of God.

Philippians 4:8 NIV *"Finally, brothers and sisters, whatever is true, whatever is noble, whatever is right, whatever is pure, whatever is lovely, whatever is admirable—if anything is excellent or praiseworthy—think about such things."*

The only way you can do this is by stopping any evil thought as soon as it comes. You can't control the thought coming, but you can control the thought continuing and forming into something more. Stop it immediately. Get up and find something active or positive to do. Or begin to read your Word and meditate on God. Pray. Go, fellowship with others. Go volunteer. Read a book. Watch a cartoon.

Whatever you have to do to refocus your mind, be intentional about it and persistent. Eventually, your mind will begin to refocus on its own, and you will change your way of thinking. You have to get up and get active or refocus it on something positive. When we don't control our thoughts, they eventually become more than an innocent fantasy but a reality.

Romans 12:12 NIV *"Do not conform to the pattern of this world, but be transformed by the renewing of your mind. Then you will be able to test and approve what God's will is—his good, pleasing and perfect will."*

Fellowship with others who are like-minded.

Ecclesiastes 4:10 NIV *"If either of them falls down, one can help the other up. But pity anyone who falls and has no one to help them up.*

If you haven't already, it is important to be a part of a group that is in line with your values, goals, and aspirations. That's honestly good to do in any aspect of your life. You need accountability in your single time, and you want to ensure to be around others who will help you in your walk and not hinder you. Find groups in your local community or church that are for singles. Connect with those who have been in your present experience to help you in your area of weakness or someone who can direct you on how they conquered their temptations.

For instance, I started a group at my job for single women that was a branch of my ministry; *Her Worth Is Far Above Rubies;* Rubies Group. It is so inspiring to fellowship and be among women who have an intimate relationship with Christ and want to please Him just as much as I do.

Conversations with others who are alike, builds your faith, gives you accountability and also helps in your times of loneliness. You gain friends, and you also gain valuable insight. Don't forsake the importance of fellowship with others. It will truly help you!

Reflection

Keep in mind that this is a short list of things to help you in your single season. Understand that you personally know what you should and should not be doing to remain faithful. We all are different and have different things that make us tick. Have some quiet time with God and ask Him to search your heart for things that you need to change. Write your own Do and Don't list! Think about times you have fallen and ways you could have prevented them. Write down what you can do next time to be better prepared. Also, write down things you will start doing to become closer to God and tap more into His strength to help you to be strong in your walk.

Isaiah 41:10 NIV *"So do not fear, for I am with you; do not be dismayed, for I am your God. I will strengthen you and help you; I will uphold you with my righteous right hand."*

The Abstinent Couple

Introduction

Being celibate is definitely a battle in itself every single day. It gets even more complicated when you get into a relationship. Why? Because you have to be not only conscious of yourself but also of your potential partner. You have to ensure you all are in sync with each other on this topic, and both have similar values and desires. The dating world for the celibate is a doozy! But don't lose faith in your desire. Though it is a tough situation, it is possible, and according to the many couples I know that did wait; it is beyond fulfilling and a blessing when you wait. The road is long, but the end result is beyond worth it.

Dating is a lot different from generations before and of course biblical times. Many didn't go through the dating process that we go through, and it has honestly made it more difficult for us to remain abstinent. In American culture, we treat dating as a trial time to figure out if we truly want to be with this mate. Sadly, during this trial period, many feel they can do things as if they are married.

But as Christians, we do not do things the world's way, but God's way. But what exactly does that look like? What can we do or not do when dating or in a relationship? What type of mate should you date in the process? What if you've have had sex before and are trying to stop now? What does that look like? The questions are endless. I am going to give you some tips on dating and also some things to refrain from if you are currently in a relationship. Also, more importantly, I am going to show the role of the male and female in helping each other remain abstinent. As always, keep in mind to make personal plans that work for you and your potential mate in conjunction with the suggestions below.

The Transitioning Couple

O kay, so you all have decided that you all want to stop having sex. I know right now it is hard to even imagine you all not being intimate with each other. How do you go from experiencing something so intimate with someone and then just stop? It's crazy even to think about it and you probably almost feel it is impossible, right? I've been there. Let me tell you about my journey with this transition.

Before I met my fiancé, I hadn't really experienced being in a mature, loving, and consistent relationship. Every relationship I'd experienced was inconsistent or immature. I never dealt with being with someone past 3 months; including my marriage. So when my fiancé and I were together, it was new for me to be with someone and not just leave the relationship when we had disagreements, or I couldn't handle not having sex. In my past relationships, if my partner and I struggled with having sex I would either just leave it, constantly go back and forth about stopping or felt it was needed for us to get married so I wouldn't have to be stressed about it. That's how I ended up in a marriage way too soon. That is not the answer. Now if you and your partner have been dating, love each other and mature, there is nothing wrong with seeking out mature counsel and seeing about your options. Most of the abstinent couples I am aware of didn't have prolonged dating periods, and I can totally understand why. But as you and your partner are dating, I have to be honest with you; it will truly take God's intervention to help you all go from a sexual to a non-sexual relationship. But it is not impossible.

Matthew 19:26 *"Jesus looked at them and said, "With man this is impossible, but with God all things are possible(NIV)."*

The relationship with my fiancé was the first I had to actually deal with my sexual urges, and it was hard. My whole life, when something was frustrating for me, I would usually just leave the situation. God had to deal with me about this flight or fight mode. If you are unsure about this concept, flight or fight is your response to a tough or difficult situation. Some people, when they are faced with a tough or fearful situation, they either leave "flight" or they stay in it and duke it out "fight". I was DEFINITELY the flightier! What's ironic is if you look at the synonyms to a flightier the words inconsistent, unreliable and erratic come up, and honestly, that was exactly how I was in my relationships. My fiancé was the first relationship where I had to deal with this issue, and I couldn't just run.

We struggled before because we had different ideas on the idea of sex before marriage. As I stated before, it is important to ensure you all are of the same mindset. It took a lot of prayers, accountability and patience for God to work on us both to do the right thing.

You may run into this issue as well with your partner. You all may have inconsistent ideas on waiting for marriage. You all are entering a new phase in your relationship and mindsets will have to change for you all to be successful. It isn't your job to change your spouse, but God's. For you all to be in one accord, it will take a lot of prayers, patience, and sacrifice. You will not be able to have the same relationship you all had before. It is a delicate situation and will have to be treated as such. You may have to stop spending the night with each other for a while, and you also may have to adjust some plans. For instance, my fiancé and I had a planned trip together, and we brought along my siblings to ensure we didn't do anything sexually. We also had to cancel some plans and change our pattern of dating. It was hard. This was really the first time I had to implement my plans with a partner. I always just avoided dealing with it. Some other things I did; I will cover in the *As A Couple* portion of this section. We had to take many of these same steps as a couple, and it worked.

You all can do this, but it will take sacrifice and a committed heart. How bad do you want to wait? How important is this for you both? If one partner seems to be struggling with the change, ensure to pray for them and have others pray for them as well. Your faithfulness to your decision will also help. But don't think it is your job to change them or force them to change. God will work on them. Until then, you ensure to stick to your decision and be a light in the relationship. It will take time. But if you all are truly for each other, love each other and committed; everything will work out perfectly.

Romans 8:28 *"And we know that in all things God works for the good of those who love him, who have been called according to his purpose.*

Woman's Role

The Power You Hold

Alright Ladies, so I know that you want to have sex with your partner just as much as he wants to be intimate with you. There is still the myth that women don't desire sex as much as men, but I am sure you can testify that is a total lie. We desire intimacy just as much as they do, and honestly, I think it is even harder for us at times because we go through loops of emotions that affect our urges, such as, our red-headed cousin that visits monthly. We go through hormonal ups and downs that can affect our need for attention and affection. We also have power over men that no other can have over them but God. You see this all the time when it comes to men and physicality. A woman can trick, and distract, a man into doing many things simply by using her looks and femininity. No matter how big or strong the man is, with the right wiles, a woman can get a man to do anything. Think about the story of Samson and Delilah. If you are unaware of the story of Samson and Delilah, Samson was a man born to save the people of Israel from the Philistines. It was prophesied to his mother that he would save the people of Israel, and he was never to drink any wine nor cut his hair. He was vowed to God and was the strongest man of the Bible. He did as God ordained for him to do; he helped to set his people free, and he did it all by the strength given to him by God.

Samson used his strength many times to kill people of the Philistines and sometimes even used his strength in unnecessary situations. Samson also had a love for Philistine women, one woman, in particular, was Delilah. Delilah was a beautiful woman, and the rulers of the Philistines used her femininity and tricks to persuade Samson to tell her the secret to his strength. Many people discuss that she would have his head laid on her lap and would coax him as she asked him where his strength lied. Samson even toyed with her and played into her game. She exclaimed that he didn't love her because he wouldn't share his secret.

Judges 16:15-16 *"Then she said to him, "How can you say, 'I love you,' when you won't confide in me? This is the third time you have made a fool of me and haven't told me the secret of your great strength." ¹⁶ With such nagging she prodded him day after day until he was sick to death of it (NIV)."*

Delilah nagged Samson about this, every single day, to a point that he finally gave in to her request. Eventually, he told her the secret to his strength, the Philistines captured him and it was the beginning of his end.

Now you have to ask yourself, how is it a woman was able to get the strongest man of his time to tell his secret? She used her ways of persuasion to get what she wanted. Now this is the thing; I am not saying that every woman uses her femininity for evil gain, but you and I both know what I am referring to when we use "wiles" to get what we want.

As women, we know what it takes to get what we want from our man. We know exactly what to say and do to get our way. Ladies, be mindful of this when it comes to your partner. You may find yourself in moments of weakness and want to persuade your man to give in to your desire. Be able to keep your mind on your goal and not use tactics to get him to fall weak to you. I know in those moments sometimes we feel so powerful. But know that your moment of power will bring him to a moment of weakness and lead to something you both regret.

Instead of using that power for weakness, use it as a way to be a light and positive persuasion to your partner. God knows the power we have over men, and He brings this power up in a way to attain positive things out of your partner. In Corinthians, God discusses a relationship where a wife may be dealing with an unbelieving spouse. He brings up the possibility of that woman's faith being a persuasion to the spouse.

1 Peter 3:1-2 *"Wives, in the same way, submit yourselves to your own husbands so that, if any of them do not believe the word, they may be won over without words by the behavior of their wives, [2] when they see the purity and reverence of your lives (NIV)."*

As you see, your behavior can have a positive influence on your partner if used for the right reasons. I know that we never have it in our minds to do such a thing to our partners, but when the flesh takes over, sometimes we go to the old tricks in the books. We don't do it in a conniving way; we just know what can make our partner melt in our hands. Which is great in the right context, but not when you are trying to wait for marriage.

Deal with Past & Insecurities

We need and love being touched by our partner and enjoy the security it gives us. Sometimes as women, especially if we are dealing with insecurities, we need physical attention to make ourselves feel wanted by our partner. We crave for that attention to make us feel secure and confident in our relationship. The key to not allowing this insecurity to control your need to be touched is to recognize the insecurity and become secure on your own.

You have to know you are loved and wanted without needing sex to prove that to you. Start asking yourself, "Why do I need my partner to touch me to make me feel wanted? Why isn't it enough that he is committed to me and in a relationship with me?" Sometimes you have to dig deep to see truly what is causing you to feel insecure or what is making you link physical attention to love. I know for me I struggled with this with guys I dated. I noticed that even with guys that did want to wait; I would find myself being utterly bothered when they didn't try to be with me physically. I didn't understand why they weren't tempted to want to be with me sexually, and when they didn't try to make an advance, it made me extremely irritated. The more this continued to happen I started asking myself, "What is our problem? Why do you have to be intimate with your partner physically?" The more and more I asked myself these questions it finally hit me.

When I first started dating seriously, I was involved with a guy who was very physically affectionate. Every chance he got he touched me, kissed me and made advances. To be honest, I loved it, and it made me feel extremely wanted. I didn't realize it at the time, but no one had ever made me feel as sexy as this man did and I was addicted to the attention. After so many advances, I eventually caved in, and he was my first. Biggest mistake of my life. But as I always tell people, God can take your mess and truly turn it into a message. If it wasn't for what I went through I wouldn't be doing what I am doing now; ministering to women.

Though I regretted the decision, I was able to look back and realize I wanted that attention because in my mind, if a man didn't want me physically then he didn't want me at all. It was odd to me when a man didn't make an advance because I equated advances to attraction. If a man didn't attempt, then to me he wasn't really interested in me or wanted me. I had to totally retrain my mind to find out what a real relationship looks like. And to realize that a relationship didn't have to involve having a sexual relationship. That a relationship could be pure, loving and intimate without sex. But it took me going back to my past and dealing with the real issue.

Right now you have some type of trained idea of what relationships consist of or you may have an insecurity that you look to a partner to secure. Whatever your internal issue may be, you have to deal with it to be able to have a healthy and pure relationship. What insecurities are controlling your relational habits?

Man's Role

A lright, my guys. Now I am not a guy, so, of course, I am limited in knowing everything you all think and go through. So I had to rack my fiancé's brain on this one. As guys, I know that it's in you all's nature to hunt and conquer. You all need sex for multiple reasons, and I know it isn't just to take advantage of a woman. That's your way of expression and your release from the day's work. You need that intimacy with your partner because you were trained to be this way. Men, you all relate physically, not emotionally, naturally. I teach communications, and one of the things I always try to explain to my students is the difference between the male and female when it comes to relationships, whether intimate or platonic. You all relate to activities; doing things with each other. Now women, on the other hand, we relate through sharing, talking and emotions. Let me give you an example.

When it's time to hang out with your buddies you all always engage in activities with each other. You may watch a game, play basketball or maybe even go to the arcade. Whatever it is, you are actively engaged in something that keeps you moving. You never call your buddy and say, "Hey Chuck, you want to come over so we can talk and catch up?" This is not natural for you guys, which is why it's hard for you to understand why ladies have to talk so much, but that's how we relate. Now women on the other hand when it's time for us to hang out we don't have to be actively doing something.

I can call a girlfriend of mine, and we can talk for hours. Or we can go to dinner and just catch up. We love talking and relating to each other. That's what helps us feel close. On the other hand, you as men, doing things physically with each other, that's what makes you feel close. The same applies to your relationships. You will naturally want to be close to your partner. You will want to touch and kiss them. You will want to conquer them and have them as your own. That is totally okay, in the right setting. Though that is your way to relate, in your relationship you will have to tap into that other part of your being to remain abstinent. Beyond finding different ways to relate, it is imperative to lead your partner and be a true helpmate.

Be A Different Kind of Active

Being active in a relationship will be good for you all, but a different kind of active. Just as you enjoy doing activities with your friends, do the same with your partner. Use this need to be physical, to actually do physical things with your partner. Go for a run. Take her to a concert. Use all of this energy to put life and energy into you all's relationship.

I understand that it may be hard for you all to just sit and talk and relate to your partner through conversation. Since you know this, do what you can to keep yourself satisfied in the relationship as well. A big part of the relationship is ultimately led by the man. Usually, he is the one who sets the tone for the relationship and how it progresses. If you want a pure relationship, you can still connect with your partner without sex. It doesn't have to be a boring relationship. To be honest, you both deciding to stop having sex will actually bring out the creative side of you. It forces you to find other things to do outside of just laying around each other's places and cuddling all the time. Explore new things with your partner. This will truly deepen you all's relationship and most of all your friendship. Relationships that have a strong foundation of friendship last longer.

You Are The Leader

God created you all to conquer. To be leaders. The same goes for your relationship with your partner. The Bible consistently talks about the man leading the woman and the woman being submissive to their spouse. Now you all may not be married, but you have been wired to lead not only your partner but your future family. Women may have a hard time admitting this sometimes, and our actions even may exude differently, but we want that leadership. We want someone who can guide us, be our strength and lead us righteously. But the key to getting us to follow is showing us we can trust you.

God even placed it this way to have order in the home. The children answer to the parents, the wife answers to the husband and the husband answers to God. It is your responsibility to present your partner pure and holy to God. Your responsibility. Many of the couples that remained abstinent required strong leadership from the man to ensure it stayed that way. Am I saying that it is solely your responsibility to ensure you all stay abstinent? No. It is both of you all's responsibility. But here is where the issue comes in. In Corinthians, Paul discusses the joys of being single and how your desires are for God and not man. When women are involved with a man, it becomes our desire to love and take care of you. It is natural for us to be loyal and committed to you and we will do anything to make you happy. Sometimes that devotion can sadly override our own needs. Now this can be a good thing when it comes to taking care of a husband and family. It truly takes a selfless love to do so. But when this love is given in an untrusting environment, we sometimes allow others needs to override our own.

Now I am not telling you this so you can take advantage of that devotion, but for you to realize this about your partner and love her tenderly and lead her the same as well. Be conscious that she needs that leadership from you and love.

That she needs you to show her you are with her in this decision and will be a leader in the decision. It is a major difference when the man is on board and ensuring to lead his partner and family righteously. The enemy is beyond aware of the importance of the man leading the family, which is why he usually attacks the man to destroy the rest of the family. He knows the man is the protector and leader of the home, and he is aware that if he can get to the man, he can get to everyone else as well. Be mindful of this. You will set the tone for your family and relationship. Are you ready?

As A Couple

Be a True Helpmate

Being a helpmate to your partner is a task that can be so fulfilling but it also takes work. For you to be able to help someone keep and attain a goal, you have to want it just as bad as they do and also care about them enough to ensure that they reach their goal. Beyond that, you have to care enough for your relationship. But for you both to reach the goal you have to train yourself to be ready for the task and be there for each other. How can you do this? You have to be prepared and aware of your weaknesses; always.

Think of it this way. Let's say you and your partner decide that you want to run a marathon together. To be able to reach this goal it will take a lot of work. You will have to train yourself physically, eat better and get yourself mentally prepared. Beyond what you do together, you have to stay accountable when you aren't around them as well. If you only prepare yourself when you are around them, but fall off course when you aren't around them, it will begin to show when you all are together as well. It's important that when you are alone to do what's needed just as if you were around them.

So what does that look like for you? I can give you a couple of things to keep in mind, but you have to know yourself and know what's best to keep you equipped and strong to stay pure in your relationship and truly be a helpmate to your partner. I will also give you some tips to be of help in the relationship.

- Don't fantasize about your partner as a way to deal with the abstinence.
- Ensure to commune with other couples who have the same goal; being celibate until marriage.
- Don't talk about fantasies or possibilities with your friends. I know we think it's okay sometimes to joke around about having sex with our partner, but the more you say it, you will begin to contemplate actually doing it.
- Stay in the Word. I find myself slipping into thoughts of sexual activity when I am also slipping in reading the Bible. Sometimes when we aren't continuously seeing what God desires of us, we forget and get distracted by the flesh. Stay in the Bible so you can have it fresh on your mind.
- Memorize Scriptures. It truly does help when scriptures come to mind to combat thoughts of the enemy.
- Stay away from sensual novels and/or movies.

- When your partner becomes weak, and you notice they are going into a sexual conversation, stop it immediately. Remind them of you all's goal and keep you all on track.
- Don't wear clothes that are too revealing of your figure or skin.
- Don't use what you know about your partner to tease them or take advantage of their weaknesses.
- If you are aware of your partner's weakness, try your best to assist them in remaining strong. For instance, if you know snuggling on the couch late at night is a weakness for them, try your best to sit on different sofas and/or simply hold hands and don't lie down.
- Be aware of your own weaknesses and do everything possible to avoid those triggers.
- Write down your personal triggers and make a plan of how you will avoid getting in that position. Be specific.
- Have scriptures written in places that will give you a reminder of your commitment to God. Keep it somewhere visible.
- Have other believers praying for you and your mate. There is power in prayer.

Write out some of your own boundaries for you and your partner.

Make a Collaborative Plan

When you have a goal to reach, you always have a plan in mind to attain it. For instance, if you want to lose weight you plan out your meals, when you will exercise, and things you will do to avoid certain foods. Just like you have plans to reach life goals you need to do the same when it comes to your decision to wait. If you don't have a plan, you will easily fall into avoidable situations, and you will also forget why you made the decision. You and your mate need to sit and make a plan together to be able to wait for marriage. Notice I said "together." It's important to do this as a collaborative effort so that both of you can voice your opinion and be a part of the plan making. The more involved you all are in making the plan, the more you will work together to sticking to the plan.

Some questions to answer in your plan:

- What time is too late for us to be together?
- What is a weak spot or weak moment for you?
- Do we always need to date in a public place?
- What triggers you to desire sex?
- Should we have accountability partners?
- Do we want to wait to travel with each other until marriage?
- What do we both need to change in our dress to help us not tempt each other?
- Is it okay for us to kiss, hold hands, etc.?
- Do we want to pray together daily on this issue?

- Can we handle spending the night with each other? If so, what are the boundaries?

There are a ton of things to consider in your planning. These are just a few questions you as a couple should answer to get the ball rolling. After you make a plan ensure to pray over it and keep it with you at all times. Combine prayer with a plan and you have a better chance at waiting until marriage. Will you be perfect? No. But you will progress and grow stronger and stronger as a couple.

Have Accountability

Just as you should have accountability and fellowship among other like-minded believers, you need to do the same in a relationship. Be around other couples who desire to date the right way. See what ways they are remaining abstinent and what works for them. Also, seek a married couple that waited until marriage. There is so much wisdom that you can attain from married couples that have walked your same journey. Find a couple you can trust and tell them about your goal as a couple. See if they are willing to meet with you together as a couple periodically to see where you all are and seek advice. Also, ask them to pray for you. It is amazing to have others praying for you all and your success.

Matthew 18: 19-20 *"Again, truly I tell you that if two of you on earth agree about anything they ask for, it will be* *done for them by my Father in heaven. [20] For where two or three gather in my name, there am I with them.""*

Fellowship with Each Other in Christ

It's so important to fellowship and worship with each other as a couple. It is a proven fact that couples that attend church regularly have longer lasting relationships compared to others who don't. It is important for you both to experience God together in Word and Worship. You all will hear the same message and be able to converse about the topics. This will help build each other's faith and relationship. Also, it's important to get involved in activities and small groups at your local church. Once again this is putting you around others who are like-minded and can help you both in your walk. Going to church together is a great habit to start as a couple and will transcend over into your family when that time comes. Embed this activity into your relationship and see it continue to flourish each day.

Save Some Activities for Marriage

When you are remaining abstinent as a couple, there will be some activities you won't be able to participate in as others do. Remember, you will have to date completely different from the world. The world's way is not conducive to a pure dating environment. Understand that what works for one couple may not work for the other.

Here are a couple of things to consider waiting to do until marriage:

- Spending the night with each other.
- Vacationing together.
- Cuddling
- Intimacy
- Having late night dinners, movie nights or dates at each other's homes.
- Kissing
- Being alone together in private places.

These are just a few activities to think about. Some may not be needed and too extreme for you, as a couple. That is totally okay. Do what you feel is best to help you wait. Sit down as a couple and decide what you would like to wait to do until marriage. Whatever you decide to wait on, it will be worth it. It will make your marriage even all the more special!

Don't Tip Toe around Sex

Some couples have their own idea of what is okay to do until marriage. There are some that believe that you shouldn't kiss while others feel that as long as you don't actually have sex that it's fine. Well, to be honest, the latter will get you into some situations that you don't want to get in. I personally tried the latter and ended up having sex with that partner. My whole life I was unaware that it was wrong to engage in foreplay. I was always told not to have sex but was never told anything else other than that. As I began to date, foreplay became a part of my first relationship, and it eventually led to sex. There was a part of me that felt something was wrong, but I was unsure and definitely didn't see it clear and cut out in the bible. The more intimate I became with Christ a lot of things became apparent to me in regards to this act.

This is what I learned in falling into the trap of foreplay.

- Anything outside of God's order is wrong. Intimacy is for you and your spouse; no one else.
- Engaging in foreplay will frustrate you and your partner, and you will eventually be tempted to have sex.
- Foreplay is just as wrong as actually having sex before marriage.
- Even if it's not plainly written out in the Bible, our Holy Spirit convicts us, and we should go with the tug of the spirit.
- You will find yourself as a couple always resulting to sexual activities when boredom occurs.
- Once you start, it's even harder to stop.
- Sex is sex.

Romans 14:23 *"...If you do anything you believe is not right, you are sinning."*

Chloe M. Gooden

Reflection

Sit down as a couple and write down your plan, the things that you want to wait until marriage to engage in as a couple, and some possible accountability partners. If you are currently in a relationship and have already fallen into some of these categories, that's okay. Pray, repent and keep moving forward. Together as a couple, you need to sit down and decide what changes need to be made to become an abstinent couple. You will definitely have to change up your current patterns. It's possible to change. As long as you have a willing heart and a connection with God, you all will be fine. Just know it will take time and a lot of change and sacrifices. But eventually it will become your normal routine, and you will be fine. It's always hard in the beginning to make a change, but get passed the tough part, and things will work out just fine.

A Letter to Abstinent Couples

I know that it can be extremely difficult to remain abstinent as a couple. Especially if one of you have experienced sex or you are transitioning into an abstinent couple. I totally understand the struggle. I dealt with this myself many times, even with my fiancé. The Lord knows our hearts and He knows that we love Him and want to do the right thing, but are sadly in the flesh. If you and your partner find yourself struggling with remaining abstinent, do whatever you feel is needed to make things right before God. Whether that means taking a step back from the relationship to slow down or pursuing the possibility of marriage.

Everyone has their own idea of what is a good amount of time to date someone before you decide to marry. I have heard of people dating for 6 weeks to 6 years before they were married. It isn't necessarily about the time, but the commitment the two have to each other. You know what you can handle and what your limits are. If you and your partner know you love each other and know for sure that you want marriage, I suggest going to speak to some pre-marital counselors. Many couples that I am aware of that were waiting for marriage didn't date for years, and honestly, I see why. Can you imagine how difficult it would be to wait to have sex with someone you have been dating for that long? Don't get me wrong; some people can do it. But you have to know yourself. If you know this is something you and your partner are struggling with; I suggest talking to a wise couple about your options as well as seek out pre-marital counseling. Speak with them about your situation and be honest about your intentions. God loves you; I know He does. I also know that He sees your heart and your desires. Do what you think is best to have peace and be right before God. He will bless your decision. Now I am in no way saying to contemplate marriage with every person you desire to be intimate with. Not saying that at all! But what I am saying is if you know you and your partner are one on this subject, love each other, have pure intentions and are trying to do the right thing, seek wise counsel. The Lord will guide you and help you all as a couple. I promise you that. He loves you, and He knows the love you have for Him and living right. Trust Him with that and trust He will give you the grace and guidance to do things right before Him. He loves you. He does care about you all as a couple. He will help you in this. I promise. God's will be done.

Advice for the Life of Celibacy & Dating

Tips for the Single, Celibate & Dating

I n this section, I have compiled some tips from males, females and abstinent couples on how to wait and date effectively. Even after reading these tips, find those around you who are waiting for marriage or waited as a couple before they were married. Talk to those you trust and you know will give you sound wisdom. I hope these tips help you in your daily walk.

Tips from the Single, Celibate & Dating

"Know your triggers. I know in my past what made me fall into temptation and where my hot spots are. I try my best to avoid those spots and ensure that I don't allow my partner to go there either" - Anonymous

"You have to be firm in your decision. Realistically, there will be someone in the relationship who may not be as strong as the other. Be able to reject them, even if it hurts

their feelings. In the end, you both will be glad you stopped."
- Anonymous

"Sexual temptation starts from the mind. When you think about it, you want to have it. Stop it there." - Anonymous

"Ensure to engage in activities that keep your mind busy and keeps you social. Tiredness, depression and loneliness sometimes have us engage in things to fill the void. Stay active and around other positive people."- Anonymous

"It's all about self-control. You have to discipline yourself to your decision. Remember why you are refraining from it and stick to it." - Anonymous

"Stay away from the sexual movies. That is usually what gets me. It gets my mind going, and I am trying my best not to go there. If a person really wants to wait, they have to be conscious of the things they watch and listen to."
- Anonymous

"Stay in prayer about your decision for celibacy. I think sometimes we forget the importance of communicating with God about situations in our lives. He will help us. But we have to stay in continued communication with him."
- Anonymous

"Have an accountability partner! So important. This may sound crazy, but my mother was mine. I don't know about you, but knowing my mother would have to ask me periodically if I had sex made me ensure I didn't do it! Couldn't imagine telling her "yes!'" - Anonymous

"Stay in the word consistently." - Anonymous

"Remember why you are doing it, and make sure you do it for yourself and not for the person you are dating."
- Anonymous

"Be around those who are on the same journey with you. Connect with other celibate friends to help you stay on track. It really does help to have supportive friends" - Anonymous

"Travel in groups. Me and my boyfriend enjoyed traveling but didn't want to slip into having sex. So we traveled with friends and ensured we stayed in the same room for accountability" - Anonymous

"Don't be discouraged by other people's opinions. Everyone has their reasoning behind their decision to have sex or not have sex. What you decide is your business and shouldn't be changed due to others opinions. You have to be strong in your belief and not be easily shaken" - Anonymous

"Use every moment to love yourself and enjoy your single life" - Anonymous

"Learn how to love yourself and put yourself first. This will help prevent you from backing down on your decision in fear of losing someone." - Anonymous

"Don't rush into the next relationship just because you're lonely." - Anonymous

"If it's obvious in the beginning the person you are dating can't handle being abstinent, you may want to re-think the possibility of a relationship. I've tried too many times getting into a relationship with others who were weak in this area, and I fell as well." - Anonymous

"Don't mope around in life because you don't have a partner. I did this for years and truly think I missed out on some exciting things in life because of this mindset. Singleness is a blessing as well. It truly is. Look at the blessings in both parts of life and don't miss all God has placed around you focusing on what you don't have." - Anonymous

"If you are struggling with remaining pure single, don't assume it will become easier with a partner. Focus on you first before trying to entertain dating." - Anonymous

"Find your purpose while you are single. Find out what God has given you to do in this world. That is where I found my fulfillment in life. I always thought that when I found a man and get married, I would have joy and feel good about life. But from one relationship to the next I realized that you can't depend on your physical surroundings for joy. When I found my calling, that's when I felt the most alive." - Anonymous

"Heal from your past hurts before getting into a relationship with anyone. I didn't heal from a lot of past

hurts before I met my boyfriend and it came up a lot in our relationship."
- Anonymous

"Don't date just anyone being desperate. Things will come out for the worst in the end." - Anonymous

"Being in a relationship now I really see the joys of singleness. I love my partner, but I truly see all of the things I could have done and worked on while I was single. Take advantage of your single season" - Anonymous

"Pray." - Anonymous

Q & A for the Single, Celibate & Dating

I usually get a lot of questions in regards to waiting on my social media pages and emails. Before writing this book, I asked my followers what questions they had in regards to being celibate and dating. As promised, I have answered the questions for them, and I hope the answers are helpful to you as well. If I have not answered a question you may have, please don't hesitate to contact me. I will glad assist you! My contact information is at the end of this guide.

Q: What if you are divorced after 20 plus years and dating again? What purpose does celibacy serve at this point?

A: I think the real question here is, "What is the purpose of celibacy?" Whether divorced or never married, celibacy is for the purpose of remaining pure until you are married under God. For God to protect a divine connection that should only be experienced with husband and wife. So if you are dating and not married to this individual, it gives God joy and protection for you to remain celibate until you all have said vows before God. I think you may be assuming that you are no longer "pure" because you have been married and have had sex. But that is not the case. Your purity doesn't change because of your marriage nor divorce. It's about being pure and righteous before God in your time of singleness and designating the act of intercourse solely for your spouse.

Q: Why does it seem hard to meet men that genuinely want only to get to know you for who you are instead of seeing you as a potential sex partner?

A: I used to feel the same way. Then I realized, maybe it isn't all men but just the men I am giving attention to. There are good men out there who want a committed relationship with you and aren't just looking for a sex partner. Now are there as many as it probably used to be? No. Our culture definitely emphasizes the sexual relationship, and you hear it in music everywhere. Sadly, this is engrained in many people's minds and affects dating. To be honest, part of the issue is that, as women, we have to stand our ground in relationships and stop allowing men to feel they are obligated to have us physically. Sometimes it starts with us! But don't give up. There truly are good men out there, but maybe you need to open your horizons. If you keep running into the same type of guys, then you may want to start evaluating what you deem as "attractive." Or possibly re-evaluate what you pay attention to when dating a guy.

Q: Since it's common that women tend to be more verbal in communication, why aren't many men more willing to listen and hear them out?

A: You are absolutely right. Women do tend to verbalize their feelings more in relationships, but men do as well, just in a different way. Men relate through activity while women relate through conversation. Though it may seem your partner isn't listening, he probably is, but it just seems he is not because he isn't responding the way you are used to. Also, it is all dependent on the guy and what he is looking for in a relationship. When I dated males who were just looking for someone to date just to pass the time, they didn't seem to be really interested in getting to know me or adjusting to making me happy. Now if it was a male who was looking for a committed relationship, it was totally different. He would attend to my needs, listen and be willing to hear me truly. If a guy is truly interested in getting to know you, and desire something long term, he will listen to you. Guarantee it.

Q: Is it okay to have a guy sleep over even if you don't plan to have sex?

A: That is a tricky one. I always tell people that you know what you can handle as well as your definition of "sleeping over" may be different from others. Is he sleeping in the same bed with you or is he sleeping on the couch? I think this goes back to knowing your triggers. Sleeping in the bed is a temptation for some and for others it may not be. Sleeping in separate rooms could also be a temptation for someone as well as to others it may not be. You want to guard yourself from being in situations that may cause you to fall. The real question is, "Do you think you can handle a man being in the bed with you without you wanting to become physical?" The enemy is a sneaky rascal and what may start off as innocent could turn into something else because you have made yourself vulnerable to the situation. Many times we fall into temptation because we didn't prevent that first step that led us there. Ask yourself, is him sleeping over going to help or hinder you in your decision to be celibate?

Also, you want to keep in mind to not do things that may appear as if you aren't following God's way. Let's say if he does sleep over and slept on the floor. But you both walk out the next morning together. Do you think those who see you will assume he slept on the floor? Probably not.

Q: When is the right time to tell someone you are dating that you want to wait for marriage?

A: I would inform them pretty early on in the relationship. Now I wouldn't tell them as soon as you all meet and yell, "Hey, I don't believe in having sex before marriage so deal with it!". But I do think it is important to inform them of your decision to wait pretty early on in those initial conversations. A good time would be when you all are getting to know each other via date or over the phone. I wouldn't do it through text. You need to voice how you feel as well as the importance of your decision. The key in doing this in person or over the phone is that you need to see and hear his response to your decision. This will tell you how he really feels about your decision. Pay attention to how he responds. Did he say, "I respect that," or did he express his thoughts and feelings about it? This is the key. Just because someone respects your decision don't assume that they understand and agree with you. They need to be in agreement with your decision and have the same belief. If they don't this will cause issues later. You need to have a serious conversation with them to ensure they are up for this decision and if they truly can do this. It's best to know this in the beginning so you won't waste their time and they don't waste yours. Don't hide that you want to wait until marriage for sex to keep a man around. It is not worth it and will only cause harm in the end.

Q: How do I bring up his relationship with God?

A: Ask him! I don't think there is anything wrong with asking a potential partner to explain their relationship with God or even ask them how they would describe their relationship and when they were saved. To be honest, you will find out more about their relationship with God in their actions more than their speech. But no one should be offended by this question. The only people that get offended are those who feel you are trying to challenge or judge how they see God. The important things are how you ask them. Maybe explain to them the importance of God in your life and the words you would use to describe Him. Then simply ask them the same thing. If they get offended, let them know that it is important to you, and you just want to get an idea of where he is as well. But honestly, you will know more about his relationship with God in the fruits he bears than the words he speaks.

Q: Is online dating okay?

A: I personally think that online dating is totally fine. Can it be dangerous sometimes? Yes. Can traditional dating be dangerous sometimes? Yes. I think you have to take precaution in dating period and take an extra step of precaution when it comes to online dating. I know many successful, married Christian couples who met online. I think the issue honestly is that people rush into relationships with others without asking the right questions and paying attention to the red flags. I talk more about this in my book *Single to Married.* Don't get online and message every person you see. Especially if you are a lady. Still allow yourself to be found. Don't hunt.

I personally enjoyed online dating because I could scan what I liked and didn't like. When you meet someone in person, you can't automatically see their level of education, if they have kids, nor what their faith is. Now some may think, "They could lie about all those things online." Well, they can lie about all those things in person too. The key is to be cautious and prayerful with anyone you meet whether via online or face to face. Many of us get in a bad situation because we rush and we aren't prayerful about those we come in contact with in the dating world. Everyone I met, whether online or traditionally, I always asked God to show me who they were from His eyes and perspective and God did it for me every time. Pay attention to what the spirit is telling you. Don't run away from that gut feeling telling you something isn't right. If you pay attention to your inner man, you will prevent a lot of issues. Be patient. Take your time. Most of all, if you are dating those online meet them in a public place. That is key! Also, take your time to speak with them online before giving your information. If you want more information on what how to date online, I have a blog at www.chloemgooden.blogspot.com that goes over this exact topic. Check it out!

Q: Me and my boyfriend slipped up and had sex. What do we do now?

A: You dust yourself off, ask for forgiveness, repent and keep moving forward with your goal! We all slip-up. Yes, I slipped up sometimes also. The key is to go back and find out what got you all to the point of slipping up and having sex. Retrace your steps and see what changes you all need to make to get back on track to your decision of remaining abstinent. Don't allow the enemy to make you think that because you slipped up it is pointless to try again. That is a lie. God knows that we make mistakes, and this is why we have grace. Receive God's grace and also receive His power to keep moving forward and remain abstinent. God will help you. Just ensure to do your part and make a plan to prevent it from happening again.

Q: How do I know when I'm ready to date again after a breakup?

A: There are a couple of things you have to factor in to ensure you are ready to date again. Some questions you may want to think about are:

Are you over your past partner?

Are you healed from any hurts that may have occurred?

Do you feel you would truly be open to meeting someone new without comparing them to your past partner?

Did you evaluate the relationship and possible changes you need to make before entering a new relationship?

I would start off with these questions to decide what's best for you. We are usually aware when we are open to meeting someone new. If you feel you aren't ready, I would definitely wait. Especially if it was a pretty serious relationship that lasted for a while or if there was a lot of damage done. Allow yourself to heal and allow yourself to enjoy singlehood. No need to rush.

Q: Is it okay to have a list for your perfect mate?

A: Definitely! Just get rid of the perfect mate part. There is no such thing. I think it is awesome to have a list of things you desire from a mate. Write down ten things you desire in a mate then circle the top three that are nonnegotiable items. These top three things may include things such as an intimate relationship with God, a leader in the home and educated. These are just examples. Ensure the list isn't shallow items such as six feet tall, has abs and fine. Write down things of importance. You don't have to worry about being attracted to your mate. You will. God will guarantee that. The most important thing to do is to write your list and then lay it before God. After I had written my list, I prayed to God,

"Lord, I desire to have a mate and if it is your will for me to have a spouse, I lay this list before you. God if there is anything that needs to change on this list, or anything I need to change, help me to be receptive to your will and trust you. You know what I need more than I do. I pray your will be done. Amen." It is totally okay to have a list. The key is to lay your list at God's feet and trust Him to bring the spouse you need.

Q: My boyfriend is okay with us deciding not to have sex, but he wants to try other stuff. What do I do?

A: You all need to have a discussion about his desires. Sex is sex. If he feels like he can't handle it, then you all may want to discuss possible options for him to handle this frustration. Many times if a man is active in sports to release any aggression it helps out. Also, ask him what are his triggers? Ensure not to do anything that may make it hard for him to resist. You don't want to engage in other sexual activities. This will lead to other things. Plus, it still is something sexual that is occurring that should be saved for the marriage bed. If it were me, I would try my best to refrain from anything sexual and discuss boundaries. You both know what you can handle and what you deem as inappropriate. If he is struggling to understand the importance of not doing anything sexual you all may want to speak with a wise couple for guidance.

Declarations, Prayers and Scriptures for the Single, Celibate & Dating

In your wait, I hope these declarations, prayers and scriptures give you a head start to know how to communicate with God and use the Word for your victory. I know it gets tough sometimes and God is ready and willing to be your strength. In each section there is a prayer you can use to communicate to God about your feelings or you can make your own. After your pray read over the scriptures as a reminder of God's faithfulness in your life. Use the Declarations to speak over your life when hard times come. I pray this guide helps you in your walk. God loves you and I do too.

Temptation

Prayer

"God, I know that with you anything is possible. I pray that you be with me in this walk with Christ, and I pray that you are always my strength, my refuge and my strong tower. Your Word says that there is no temptation that has come over me that isn't common to man. That you are faithful and will always provide a way of escape. I pray you not only provide a way of escape, but you help me be sensitive to the Holy Spirit's guidance as well. Lord, I desire to be pleasing to your sight, and I need your help to do so. Sustain me, as you've promised. Be my strength in my weaknesses, as you've promised. Walk with me, as you've promised. I know I can do this with you, God. Thank you, Lord, for victory and thank you for your grace and mercy even if I fall. Nothing can separate us from your love, and I pray that I always remember that. Thank you for being with me every step of the way. I love you, God. Amen."

Declaration

I have victory through Christ Jesus.
I am pure in mind, body, spirit and soul.
My mind is renewed daily.
My spirit is stronger than my flesh.
Where I am weak God makes me strong.
Nothing is worth separation from God.
God will always provide me with a way of escape.

I am connected to the Divine Power within me to be sustained and victorious in this walk.

Scriptures

2 Corinthians 12:9
"My grace is sufficient for thee, for my strength is made perfect in weakness."

2 Timothy 4:17
"The Lord stood with me, and strengthened me."

Galatians 5: 16-18
"So I say, walk by the Spirit, and you will not gratify the desires of the flesh. For the flesh desires what is contrary to the Spirit, and the Spirit what is contrary to the flesh. They are in conflict with each other, so that you are not to do whatever[c] you want. But if you are led by the Spirit, you are not under the law."

1 Corinthians 10:13
"No temptation has seized you except what is common to man. And God is faithful; he will not let you be tempted beyond what you can bear. But when you are tempted, he will also provide a way out so that you can stand up under it."

1 Corinthians 6:18
"Flee from sexual immorality. All other sins a man commits are outside his body, but he who sins sexually sins against his own body."

Matthew 26:41

"Watch and pray so that you will not fall into temptation. The spirit is willing, but the body is weak."

Psalm 119:9-10

"How can a young man keep his way pure? By living according to your word. I seek you with all my heart; do not let me stray from your commands."

Psalm 119:11

"I have hidden your word in my heart that I might not sin against you."

1 Peter 5:8-9

"Be self-controlled and alert. Your enemy the devil prowls around like a roaring lion looking for someone to devour. Resist him, standing firm in the faith, because you know that your brothers throughout the world are undergoing the same kind of sufferings."

Strength & Hope in Your Sacrifice

Prayer

"God, sometimes in this walk I get frustrated and discouraged. I want to be pleasing to your sight, but sometimes it feels pointless and hopeless. I see others around me attaining what they desire as I sit here and try my best to be obedient to your Word. God remind me of the importance of waiting. Help me to see that my present sacrifices don't compare to the glory revealed later. Keep me from giving up on this journey. Lord, I need a fresh reminder that I will reap my desires if I faint not. Be with me. Strengthen me. Remove any doubts or fears from the enemy from my spirit and/or surroundings. Lord fill my cup with your love, assurance and strength to keep moving forward. Amen."

Declaration

God will honor my sacrifices.
The sacrifices of my present time do not compare to the reward at the end.
God is strengthening me daily.
He sees me. He sees my heart and sacrifices.
My love for God and God's love for me outweighs the hard times.
My walk will be a testimony to other singles and couples.
I am a light.
God will never give up on me, and I will never give up on Him.

Scriptures

Galations 6: 9
"Let us not become weary in doing good, for at the proper time, we will reap a harvest if we do not give up."

Romans 8:18
"I consider that our present sufferings are not worth comparing with the glory that will be revealed in us."

James 1:2-4
"Consider it pure joy, my brothers, whenever you face trials of many kinds, because you know that the testing of your faith develops perseverance. Perseverance must finish its work so that you may be mature and complete, not lacking anything."

Romans 5: 3-5
"And not only this, but we also exult in our tribulations, knowing that tribulation brings about perseverance; and *perseverance, proven character; and proven character, hope; and hope does not disappoint, because the love of God has been poured out within our hearts through the Holy Spirit who was given to us."*

Psalm 39:7
"Now, Lord, what do I look for? My hope is in you."

Psalm 43:5
" Why are you downcast, O my soul? Why so disturbed within me? Put your hope in God, for I will yet praise him, my Savior and my God."

James 1: 12

"Happy is the man who doesn't give in and do wrong when he is tempted, for afterward he will get as his reward the crown of life that God has promised those who love him."

Romans 12:12

"Be joyful in hope, patient in affliction, faithful in prayer."

Contentment

Prayer

"Lord, though I am grateful for the many things you've given me, I do find myself being envious of those who are married or living in ways, not of you. It seems that there are those who are not living by your Word and receiving what they desire, and it also seems everyone around me is in a secure relationship. I desire these things and feel disappointed when I see I still don't have it. Sometimes it makes me feel as if you are not here. I begin to question if you hear my prayers or if you even care. Lord, forgive me if I seem ungrateful; I am not. It is just hard to see others with what I desire. God help me to be content with what you have given me and accept the season you have me in currently. To every season there is a blessing and my singleness is a blessing, not a curse. Lord help me to take hold of this time to draw closer to you and work on myself. Amen."

Declaration

I am blessed beyond measure.
The life you have given me was designed specifically by your hands, and it is perfect.
I have everything I need.
You hear my every prayer and request.
You know not only my needs but also the secret petitions of my heart.

I will have the desires of my heart in due time.

God is faithful to His promises.

I am at peace.

I have joy.

I am content.

Scriptures

Philippians 4: 11-12

"I have learned to be content whatever the circumstances. I know what it is to be in need, and I know what it is to have plenty. I have learned the secret of being content in any and every situation, whether well-fed or hungry, whether living in plenty or in want."

Psalm 37: 7-9

"Be still before the Lord and wait patiently for him; do not fret when men succeed in their ways when they care out their wicked schemes. Refrain from anger and turn from wrath; do not fret-it leads only to evil. For evil men will be cut off, but those who hope in the lord will inherit the land."

Proverbs 24:19

"Do not fret because of evildoers or be envious of the wicked..."

Ecclesiastes 3:1

"There is an appointed time for everything. And there is a time for every event under heaven— "

1 Corinthians 7:17
"Each one should retain the place in life that the Lord assigned to him and to which God has called him."

Patience

Prayer

"Lord, sometimes it's truly frustrating waiting on you in this time of singleness. I know you have the best intentions for me in mind, but it just feels things are taking forever. God, please help me to wait on the best you have for me and not desperately fall into bad situations and relationships to fill the void. God help me to be strong in my wait and also accept what your will is for my life. I don't know if it is your will for me to marry, but I do pray in the wait you allow me to be strong, joyful and content. Lord help me wait on you, Lord. Help me to see the light at the end. In Jesus Name. Amen."

Declaration

My God knows what's best for me.
My wait doesn't compare to what God has in store for me.
I am patient. I am at peace. I am content.
The Lord is renewing my strength every day.
I am patient. I have peace. He is with me.
His will is far greater than my own.

<u>*Scriptures*</u>

Isaiah 40:31
"But those who wait on the Lord Shall renew their strength; They shall mount up with wings like eagles, they shall run and not be weary, they shall walk and not faint."

Proverbs 14:29
" Whoever is patient has great understanding, but one who is quick-tempered displays folly."

Romans 12:12
"Be joyful in hope, patient in affliction, faithful in prayer."

Galations 6:9
"Let us not become weary in doing good, for at the proper time, we will reap a harvest if we do not give up."

Psalm 27:14
"Wait for the Lord; be strong and take heart and wait for the Lord."

Psalm 37:7
"Be still before the Lord and wait patiently for him; do not fret when people succeed in their ways when they carry out their wicked schemes."

God's Faithfulness

Prayer

"God, sometimes I feel you don't hear me and my situation will never change. I struggle with the life of being celibate and dating and it feels I will never amount to who you've called me to be. Lord, I feel you aren't here with me sometimes. Please remind me of your faithfulness. Remind me that you see and hear everything. Help me to see reflections of you in every area of my life. Give me a spirit of peace and assurance that you are always here and continuously strengthening and loving me. You are a faithful God. Remind me of this every time I doubt you are."

Declaration

God is always with me.
He promises to never leave nor forsake me.
He hears my every prayer.
I am covered.
I am loved.
I am restored.
Everything I need, God is providing.
He is forever faithful.

Chloe M. Gooden

Scriptures

Numbers 23:19

"God is not human, that he should lie, not a human being, that he should change his mind. Does he speak and then not act? Does he promise and not fulfill? (NIV)"

Lamentations 3: 22-23

"Through the Lord's mercies we are not consumed, because his compassions fail not. They are new every morning; Great is Your faithfulness(NKJV)."

Psalm 57:10

"For great is your love, reaching to the heavens; your faithfulness reaches to the skies(NIV)."

It's Your Decision

We all have choices in this life. Regardless of anything you may read, or hear, you will make up in your mind what you want to do and whether or not you want to wait for marriage to have sex. Whether because it is a struggle for you, or you just don't believe in it, we all have our reasons for why we make the decisions we do. I am in no way judging whatever decision you make but do understand that every choice comes with a consequence. Everything we do affects us in some way. I already went over some of those effects so whatever decision you decide to make; you know what comes with it. I struggled with waiting myself. Not because I didn't believe in it, but because it was a struggle to stop after I'd started. I wrestled with this for years and many times didn't have peace in my life. My heart was right, but I was human, and I struggled. I spoke with my father about this, and he gave me an answer I am so grateful for till this day. I hope this same response will give you peace as well. I love you. God loves you. I pray He gives you strength to make the right decision and to walk out His will.

Rev. Herbert Gooden Jr.

"To this day, we know that sin limits you not God. God does not punish. There is a reward for living toward righteousness. No one is perfect, but we have the power to choose. God does not change. We are saved by grace. Romans Chapter 6 is explicit about this subject. You need to keep this in mind. God does not get mad or punish us. That's Old Testament thinking. We limit him and His spirit acting in us by our thoughts and action or inaction. In other words, it delays blessing in certain areas of our lives."

It's Your Decision.

About The Author

Chloe M. Gooden is a mentor, speaker, and author of *Not Tonight: My Worth Is Far Above Rubies, Single to Married and Single to Married Devotional.* She has spoken at several events on the life of celibacy, sexual temptation, dating, and relationships. She is the creator and manager of Her Worth Is Far Above Rubies, a community focused on encouraging women in life, dating, relationships and knowing their worth. She is from Birmingham, Alabama and graduated from Mississippi State University with her Bachelors and the University of Alabama at Birmingham for her Masters. Her passion is to encourage and enlighten others through God's Word. She hopes to continue helping others to develop an intimate relationship with Christ and help women see their worth, find their calling and live the amazing, free and healed life God intended for them to live.

CONNECT WITH US

Chloe M. Gooden

Facebook: Chloe M. Gooden
Instagram: @chloemgooden
Twitter: @chloemgooden

Her Worth is Far Above Rubies

Facebook: Her Worth Is Far Above Rubies
Instagram: @knowyourworthrubies
Twitter: @AboveRubiesUR

www.chloemgooden.com

THANKS FOR READING!
WE INVITE YOU TO SHARE YOUR
THOUGHTS AND REACTIONS!

OTHER BOOKS BY CHLOE M. GOODEN

Single to Married: Becoming Who You Are In Christ and a Better Complement as a Potential Wife

Become a better you and be ready to take on dating, relationships, and marriage. You cannot be a complement to someone until you are complete in Christ.

Single to Married exposes major mistakes of the single woman in dating and relationships. Helps you make better choices in choosing a mate. Opens your eyes to everything that marriage, and being a wife, truly encompasses. Guides you in finding who you are and who God has called you to be. Shows you how to receive the life of fulfillment through healing, restoration, and a relationship with Christ.

OTHER BOOKS BY CHLOE M. GOODEN

Single to Married Devotional

30 Days of Transformation, Restoration, and Healing

Get the perfect companion guide to Single to Married and be guided in prayer and reflection. Helping you transform in being whole in Christ!

Single to Married Devotional gives you a 30-day prayer starter and reflection to help you work through emotional, relational, and spiritual battles and hardships. This devotional is the perfect companion to your Single to Married reading to help you become the woman that God formed you to be: Healed, Transformed, and Restored.

Made in the USA
Coppell, TX
15 September 2020

37978009R00079